IGNITE
— YOUR —
SUPER
SIGHT

THE POWER OF SPIRITUAL VISION TO FUEL
YOUR FUTURE AND MOVE MOUNTAINS

JULIA KITZ

First Edition, August 2023

ISBN: 979-8-9886603-0-9 (paperback)
ISBN: 979-8-9886603-1-6 (ebook)

Vision 2 Victory
Cincinnati, Ohio, U.S.A.

vision2victory.org

To every believer brave enough to seek (and even find) more of God.

JULIA KITZ

"So we fix our eyes not on what is seen, but on what is unseen, since what is seen is temporary, but what is unseen is eternal."

(2 Corinthians 4:18 NIV)

Contents

Introduction   1

1. THE DIVINE FILTER   3

2. EIGHT ELEMENTS OF SPIRITUAL VISION   19

3. THE SECRETS OF THE SEERS   29

4. ILLUMINATING THE WAY   41

5. IN STEP WITH THE SPIRIT   49

6. DIVINE INDWELLING   55

7. PURE PASSION   61

8. THE VIEW FROM ABOVE   67

9. EMPOWERED FOR MORE   73

10. ENVISION THE PROVISION   79

11. PEACE FROM ANOTHER PLACE   85

12. VARYING VIEWPOINTS   91

13. TWELVE KEYS THAT UNLOCK SPIRITUAL VISION   101

Acknowledgements   135

Appendix - Resources   137

Introduction

I used to think Christians were different, even weird, at times. Going to church never made much sense to me, and religion seemed like a means of escape for many people. Fast-forward to my thirties, I accepted Christ into my heart and began the journey as a Jesus follower.

Life was fairly good. I was reading the Bible and attending various classes and events at church, yet I still felt like an imposter. It always felt as if the "other" Christians were authentic, but I was a phony. Other believers appeared to have something I was missing, but I couldn't quite put my finger on it. Sometimes they shouted with joy, lifted their hands, and even *cried!* (gasp!) Some even talked about having conversations with God, feeling the Holy Spirit move, or having divine visions, dreams, or encounters. They seemed in tune with God in a way that I wasn't.

"What's wrong with me?" I thought. "Maybe I'm not really a Christian after all. Maybe this is all just a lie."

Surely I'm not the only person who has sat in a sanctuary full of people but still felt alone, different, or not quite enough. I later realized my insecurity was normal, and that though my feelings were real, the thoughts that triggered them were untrue. My vision was just clouded! Once I focused on keeping my spiritual eyes open, I was able to start seeing through God's lens. I was able to clearly see my identity, my purpose, my gifts, and my hope-filled future.

Reaching the bare minimum in faith is a choice. Doing something significant for Jesus and His Kingdom is also a choice. You're about to discover what your *spiritual* eyes can see that your *physical* eyes cannot. You'll learn how to see what God wants you to see.

If you're struggling to find your groove with God or feel you're missing a piece of this pie called religion, learning how to ignite your supernatural sight can make all the difference. As you begin to view life through the eyes of your spirit, you will find power to fuel your future and move mountains!

Chapter 1

THE DIVINE FILTER

Like many believers today, you may be familiar with the expression **"mountain-moving faith."** This phrase is in reference to Jesus' teachings to His disciples in the gospel accounts. On one occasion, we find Jesus responding to His disciples' inability to expel a demon from a boy, despite their continued efforts. The disciples ask the Lord why they couldn't cast out the demon themselves. He responds by saying,

> *"You don't have enough faith," Jesus told them. "I tell you the truth, if you had **faith** even as small as a mustard seed, you could say to this **mountain**, 'Move from here to there,' and it would **move**. Nothing would be impossible"* (Matthew 17:20 NLT emphasis added).

Another time, Jesus sees a fig tree full of leaves yet it's without fruit. He speaks to the fig tree, and it withers away. The disciples are amazed. The Lord responds again by explaining that if they would have faith, even a *mountain* can be lifted and thrown into the sea. He tells the disciples that if they believe what they say, they will receive. Again, the example was a mountain being moved (Matthew 21:20-21, Mark 11:23).

We can conclude from these examples that there is an effective two-fold spiritual principle in operation causing things to happen: *belief* coupled with *speech.* If we can begin to genuinely believe that our prayers and our Holy Spirit-inspired speech are indeed working, we will begin to see our giant "mountains" of unfruitful, challenging, or negative aspects of our lives removed from our paths.

So, what does all this have to do with spiritual sight? I'm so glad you asked! I'd like to propose that an important *third* part of the belief plus speech equation is *vision.*

How much more effective and fruitful could our lives be if we not only lived full of faith and the word of God but also filled with supernatural vision? Vision that sees the result *before* the request. Vision that sees the answer *before* the prayer. Vision that sees the unobstructed path ahead even while the mountain is still in full view. The power of spiritual vision can fuel our future as we visualize the mountains in our lives removed. We can ascend the spiritual heights God has envisioned for us by opening our supernatural eyes.

The key is keeping our eyes off the mountain and focused on God. The Apostle Peter was only able to walk on water while he focused on Jesus. As soon as Peter fixated on the wind and waves around him, instead of the Lord, fear came. Consequently, he began to sink into the water (Matthew 14: 29-30). Our faith or our fear can be activated by our spiritual sight and imagination. Living in faith is envisioning a future where God is with us. Living in fear is visualizing a future without God.

We are designed to envision what we are looking forward to. Peering through the divine filter of faith allows us to perceive things the way God does. As a follower of Jesus, in whom you believe but probably have not yet seen, you have already embarked on a supernatural visionary journey! As you learn to take your spiritual vision to new heights, you will be joining the heroes of faith that were able to see *from a distance* the promises of God despite their current circumstances, conditions, or mountains. Sharpening your divine sight will reveal a life-changing relationship with the mountain-moving God!

BLIND BUT NOW I SEE

Encountering Jesus outside our Bibles, prayers, and worship playlists sometimes feels like a gene you either have or you don't. Some get visions and dreams, others heal people miraculously, and then the rest…well, we still believe. We may even chase after those encounters, hoping we're not subconsciously manufacturing them ourselves.

Nevertheless, every believer *can* experience God in those supernatural, beyond-explanation ways. More than that, believers can learn to recognize and encounter this beautiful empowerment in God. It takes a spiritual breakthrough in our eyesight and insight to get there, but *all* followers are in His presence and have the same opportunity to see Him in amazing ways.

You may have been reading and studying the Bible for years. Perhaps you have learned how to pray and believe God's Word. Maybe you have even received divine healing and now pray for others. However, if you're anything like I was, you have yet to see the type of encounters with God you've read about in the Bible. I wanted to see and hear the types of things the prophets and the disciples did! I asked the Holy Spirit to bring the Word to life in new ways.

So began my quest for a naturally supernatural lifestyle. My husband, Scott, and I began attending a local church that emphasized the work of the Holy Spirit and spiritual giftings as an everyday part of a believer's life.

After we had attended that new church for a little over a month, I felt more alive in my spirit than I had in a long time. We began attending several of the church's classes. We soon became involved in the prayer team and even began praying for people at the local shopping mall. These were all the things that I had desired to do but didn't know how to begin. As I began to help others, God began to open my spiritual eyes and ears to see and hear more from Him. **I was beginning to find *supernatural* vision in an *ordinary* world!**

Amazingly, I began having some spiritual visions. In other words, as my eyes were closed, I could see images, pictures, and film-like scenes in my mind. It was as if I was having a dream, but I was awake. At that point, everything about my relationship with God changed magnificently. As you, too, learn to visualize the Kingdom and Jesus' victory, you will attain more breakthroughs in your life.

Even if you're not particularly desiring divine visions and encounters, *everyone* can benefit from clarifying God's vision for their life. Learning how to envision yourself and others as God does will improve your relationships. Visualizing your future will positively impact your life trajectory. Perhaps you've never experienced a vision like John, Daniel, or others in the Bible. That's perfectly okay. You can start by focusing on God's vision for your future and go from there.

Though I can't rush or force your spiritual journey and mindset, I also encourage you to explore your own privilege and opportunity to hear from and understand God through the Holy Spirit. Use my experience as a launching point for how to clarify your vision and help others in the process.

Our faith and relationship with God can always be deeper. We may never comprehend all the knowledge about God while on this earth. However, the things God has prepared for His children in heaven and eternity are now *made visible and revealed to us by the Holy Spirit* (1 Corinthians 2:7-10). **We can all believe to see the fulfillment of God's promises in our lives**.

GOD'S LENS

Visions can have many sources. An organization may write a vision statement after collaborating with coworkers. A sporting team may create a vision for their team. However, the average person does not seem to form much of a vision for their future. As Jesus' followers, we are not ordinary. We are extraordinary! As such, when we seek to clarify our spiritual sight, move in faith, and envision our mountains moving, we partner with the Holy Spirit.

Scripture reminds us that where there is no vision, people perish (Proverbs 29:18). To perish means to decline, decay, or die. With no clear vision, individuals and organizations are indecisive or confused about their mission. Time is wasted and opportunities can be missed. That's the last thing we want as people of God! We want to grow, increase, flourish, and live the abundant life that Jesus died for us to have. Therefore, it's essential to have an unobstructed vision of God's plan and purpose for our lives.

God reveals His vision for His children throughout the Bible. But God also has a unique vision *of* you and *for* you. Yet many times we come up with our own vision. Then after we pursue it, we ask God to bless it. However, God tends to reveal His vision to us over time. As we take one step of faith and obedience, God will tell us what the next step is.

In the book of Genesis, God had a clear vision of blessing the nation of Israel through Abraham. Yet all He told Abraham at first was to leave his home and head out for a place that God would show him. It wasn't until after Abraham had taken that first step at the Lord's prompting that God shared His vision with Abraham. God later revealed His full vision for Abraham and for Israel, but it required listening to God and responding with steps of faith and obedience first.

Likewise, when Jesus called the disciples, He simply asked them to stop what they were doing and to follow Him instead. As they listened and responded with steps of faith and obedience, Jesus later revealed more details about His vision with the disciples. They only saw part of the Lord's vision, but as they responded to Jesus, the vision became clearer to them. In both instances, God not only revealed *His* vision but also the vision He had for Abraham and the disciples.

It would do us much good to learn how to see through God's lens (how He sees us, others, and the situations we find ourselves in). While we tend to look at outward appearances, God looks at the heart. He does not see as we see (1 Samuel 16:7). Visualizing how God sees others nurtures our relationships. As we begin to see people through the lens of God's love, we will see others according to their potential, not their past.

God has a unique frequency with which He wants to communicate and share His vision with you. As you learn how to tune into the realm of heaven, you will be able to see with your spiritual sight more clearly and from a higher perspective.

Envisioning the world through the Holy Spirit's filter doesn't happen overnight. But as you progressively pursue God's vision for yourself, you will begin to see how God is actively engaged in fulfilling *His* vision through *you.*

THE SPIRITUAL SENSES

Our spiritual senses are just as active and perceptive as our natural and physical senses. The same way we know someone is coming near us through our auditory abilities (as well as visual), we have spiritual senses that communicate with us about God. With our outer vision, we see physical realities. With our inner vision, we see spiritual realities. Likewise, we hear physical noises with our outer ears but hear God's voice with our spiritual ears.

God is a Spirit. We are made in His image, and the Holy Spirit indwells us when we accept Him into our lives. In this way, He can communicate to us through our spirits (John 4:24). When we become children of God, we receive a new, spiritual heart. We are made into new creations. Having been filled with the Holy Spirit, we hear the spiritual language of God. He can speak in thoughts, words, images, visions, dreams, and much more our human minds cannot imagine.

The Apostle Paul prayed that the Ephesians would have their spiritual eyes *opened* so they would experience a full revelation of the hope, calling, and inheritance that is found in God through Jesus Christ (Ephesians 1:18).

This is also what Jesus meant when He spoke of those who have *eyes to see* in Matthew 13:15-16.

Our spiritual eyes allow us to perceive spiritual realities. Like the wind, sometimes we do not notice this sense unless it is powerful enough to move tree branches. Spiritual senses can also seem hidden like the sun on dark winter days, perhaps from our own fog or an obstruction by the enemy, Satan. However, just because we can't see the sun with our physical eyes every moment, it's still in the sky, hidden behind the clouds.

Even non-believers have spiritual senses and believe in a spirit world to a certain extent. In the early 2000s, the phrasing of some people's beliefs as "spiritual but not religious" became popularized by author Sven Erlandson. Someone who identifies as spiritual but not religious feels a greater presence in the world but does not identify it with a specific organized religion or belief system. Certainly, this could be our spiritual senses desiring God but not yet awakened to His voice. I also think of the many times I've met or been told of people with mental illness who hear voices that no one else hears or can source. Those aren't physical voices but could be spiritual demonic voices.

During my prayer time one day, I felt like the Lord said, "People believe that the enemy can speak to them more than I can!" That really convicted me to start believing that I could hear God clearly in my mind and with my spirit. Many people in the Bible grew in faith and knowledge through dreams and visions (Moses, Daniel, Zechariah, Mary, etc.). Certainly if the enemy can put thoughts into our minds, our loving Father and Lord can speak to us there too. This is what Paul meant when he prayed that the eyes of our hearts (or understanding) would be *enlightened*.

Some in the body of Christ see the spiritual world even with their physical eyes open. They can see Jesus, angels, and demons within their physical context. Most who do have been able to since childhood. I do not have that gift (at least not to my knowledge). I can, however, see with my spiritual eyes. This means I get pictures, images, visions, and film-like scenes in my mind with my eyes usually closed. Some people might think that is just my imagination, as I did initially. However, Paul reminds us that it is more than imagination:

*"So we fix our eyes not on what is **seen**, but on what is **unseen**, since what is seen is temporary, but what is unseen is eternal"* (2 Corinthians 4:18 NIV, emphasis added).

The Amplified Version translates it in this powerful way:

*"So we look not at the things which are **seen**, but at the things which are **unseen**; for the things which are visible are temporal [just brief and fleeting], but the things which are **invisible** are everlasting and imperishable"* (emphasis added).

Many of the Old Testament prophets and New Testament believers saw with the eyes of their spirits also. Perhaps God is challenging you to begin noticing not only what you see physically but what you might be able to see spiritually. The Holy Spirit may want to reveal more to you through your spiritual eyesight or your inner voice.

A FASHIONED IMAGINATION

When people become Christians, they are saved from their sins and from death by God's grace because they have *faith* in who He is. Hebrews 6:12 tells us that through *faith* and patience, we inherit the promises of God. Faith means unwavering, confident belief. Faith is often a result, to some extent, of our spiritual development and vision. Our faith grows as we *envision* the promises of God.

A visionary lifestyle requires us to elevate our faith using what God says and what we picture inside. God's Word includes powerful imagery and detail sometimes, but especially at first, it might not seem like enough. Without a capability to *visualize* Scripture and imagine it how we perceive it, we miss the opportunity to grow our faith in God's promises and truth.

God has a purpose for our imagination. As believers, we can use our imagination to activate our faith. Faith requires that we believe *before* we see.

Followers of Jesus have been transformed, so we are no longer just human beings. As we develop a *"sanctified" imagination* (in other words, divinely inspired thoughts), we begin to see through a new lens of spiritual sight that looks beyond our natural experiences to the promises of God! To "sanctify" something means to set it apart for unique use or to make it holy. As we meditate on the scriptures, we become transformed into God's likeness in our thinking. We have full access to the mind of Christ and can pursue the sanctification process in our minds, thinking, and imagination by faith and by reading God's Word.

A *sanctified* imagination is not the same as the Law of Attraction or the concept of manifestation. Rather, it is the presence of the Holy Spirit in us perceiving the unseen realm. As we yield our imaginations to the Holy Spirit, our thoughts and imaginings will become progressively sanctified. Our thoughts, reasonings, and imaginations continue to come under the authority of Christ (2 Corinthians 10:5). This is accomplished by a total reformation of how we think (Romans 12:2). A sanctified imagination can receive messages, dreams, and visions from God. Human reasoning might change our minds, but a sanctified imagination can change our hearts!

The problem many Christians have is not an *overactive* imagination, but an *underactive* imagination. As we learn to develop a healthy imagination, we will be able to perceive what is vital and valuable. Our heavenly Father gets excited when we see in faith what we do not yet possess in the natural! God is visionary, and He desires us to be people who can visualize as well.

The word "imagination" is *yasar* in Hebrew and *dianoia* in Greek. The noun y*asar* means "to form or to fashion" and is the exact same word that describes how God created man! We read,

> "*Then the Lord God **formed*** (yasar) *man from the dust of the ground and breathed into his nostrils the breath of life, and the man became a living being*" (Genesis 2:7 NIV, emphasis and Hebrew *yasar* added).

God imagined and formed us first, so when we imagine (or "behold forms") in our mind or thinking, we are acting like our Creator!

David wrote in one Psalm,

> "*Your eyes saw my substance, being yet unformed. And in Your book they all were written, the days **fashioned*** (yasar) *for me, When as yet there were none of them.*"

(Psalm 139:16 NKJV, emphasis and Hebrew *yasar* added).

Here, the same verb for "to form or to fashion" is used to describe how God has already planned the days of our lives. As we live here on the earth, every day of our lives can bring a fresh vision, a fresh form to behold, or a fresh way of thinking!

The Greek word translated as "imagination," "understanding," or "mind" is *dianoia.* It's a combination of the two words *dia* (by or through) and *nous* (the mind or intellect). In other words, we imagine by or through our minds, intellect, understanding, and thinking. This is what Paul was referring to when he prayed for the church to have supernatural revelation. He prayed that the church would open the eyes of their hearts, understanding and *imagining* so as to be flooded with light.

Paul also reminds us through his epistle to the Romans to *continue* opening our eyes. Even the most mature and wise believers need renewed and refreshed minds through God and not through man or changing culture. By doing so, our imaginations stay God-centered, Jesus-focused, and Holy Spirit-inspired.

We encounter and attain every blessing found in the Bible when we have strong faith empowered through God's grace. It is through believing in the biblical promises that we will be able to have spiritually inspired dreams, encounters, and visions! I just love the verse in Isaiah 30:18 that promises us:

*"And therefore the Lord [earnestly] waits [expecting, looking, and longing] to be gracious to you; and therefore He lifts Himself up, that He may have mercy on you and show loving-kindness to you. For the Lord is a God of justice. Blessed (happy, fortunate, to be envied) are all those who [earnestly] wait for Him, who **expect and look** and long for Him [for His victory, His favor, His love, His peace, His joy, and His matchless, unbroken companionship]!"* (AMPC, emphasis added).

As believers, we aim to become fully persuaded in faith (not doubt) about the decisions we make, large or small. God is so good. He will give us what we ask of Him if we ask in faith without doubting (James 1:6). If you are ready for more evidence of God's voice and vision in your life, then I encourage you to say the following prayer with me:

Father, help me to see through my eyes of faith. I want to see, hear, and experience You more. I am choosing to see You and Your goodness in the here and now. I want to follow Your vision for my life. I want to see more clearly with the eyes of my heart, hear with the ears of my spirit, and activate my faith with my imagination. I choose to believe before I see, visualizing Your Word and promises concerning me. I declare that the eyes of my understanding are flooded with revelation light, according to Your Word. That supernatural knowledge is helping me to know You more and to know the purpose and power that I have in You as Your child. When You formed me, You also formed my mind. I dedicate myself to renewing my mind according to Your Word. I offer my complete self, including my eyes, my ears, my mind, and my imagination to You. In Jesus' name. Amen.

Chapter 2

EIGHT ELEMENTS OF SPIRITUAL VISION

A *vision* can imply many things. It can be the state of seeing literally with *physical sight*. It can also refer to the ability to see figuratively with *spiritual sight.* A vision can be a vivid mental image of the present or future. It can be the ability to envision the future with our imaginations. A vision can also be an experience of someone or something in the mind—a dream or a trance.

We can receive a *divine vision* by reading Scripture, hearing God's voice, sensing the prompting of the Holy Spirit, or by having a divine encounter or dream. A vision can be something that God puts in us, or it can be something we see on purpose with God's input and leading. Visions give us passion and direction. This is why many individuals, teams, and organizations form vision statements. For some, that will be a sentence, a story, or a picture in their minds. Regardless, visions help us picture the future with hope, purpose, and faith.

Clarity of vision concerning the key facets of our lives builds wisdom. Having an unclouded vision for ourselves, our families, our careers, our business, our community, or our ministry is important. This is because vision creates energy and direction. Vision helps us establish priorities and set goals in certain areas of our lives. Vision will ensure that we discern our divine appointments and assignments.

Jesus was able to fully see and participate in the Father's vision. He pursued God's plan of redeeming humanity through Himself as He journeyed from the cradle to the cross.

EIGHT ELEMENTS OF SPIRITUAL VISION

Sharpened vision helps us maintain focus and gives us insight into key areas of our lives. The eight elements of spiritual vision will provide answers to questions such as:

- **Purpose** – What am I here for and what has God planned for my life?

- **Position** – Which direction is my life taking and is it part of God's plan?

- **Presence** – How can I feel closer to God and sense the leading of the Holy Spirit?

- **Passion** – Where can I find more energy and joy in my life?

- **Perspective** – How can I view my circumstances and challenges differently?

- **Power** – Where will I find the strength and ability to do what God asks of me?

- **Provision** – How will God meet my needs abundantly?

- **Peace** – How can I find more contentment and satisfaction in my life?

Having a clear spiritual vision can transform and define us by revealing how God sees us. His vision for our lives is bigger than we can even imagine; so much so that it may seem impossible to attain when we discover it. It will take our eyes of faith and God's grace to achieve. As such, God will get *all* the credit when He accomplishes His purpose through us. This brings us to the first element of supernatural vision, which is purpose.

1. Purpose

Vision gives us purpose for our lives, and having a purpose in what we are doing excites us, energizing us for the path it requires. Vision motivates us. It prompts action. It releases our imagination. When God inspires us with a vision, it's an opportunity for us to become more for God. It's a way for us to accomplish something in our lives that will bless God and others. As we stay focused on Christ and follow Him, our purpose will come into view.

Jesus knew exactly what His purpose and mission on the earth were. He told the tax collector, Zacchaeus, that He was sent to seek and save the lost people of Israel, coming down from heaven to do the will of the Father who sent Him (Luke 19:10; John 6:38).

When Jesus appeared to His disciples after His resurrection, He reminded them that *His purpose* was *their purpose*. As the Father sent Him, He was sending them (John 20:21). As followers of Jesus, pursuing *His* vision will give our lives more meaning and purpose.

2. Position

Vision gives us a supernatural roadmap. It will keep us in the right position and help us head in the right direction. We can decide where and when we should focus our attention with better discernment, which helps us pursue or decline what does not contribute to that path. Vision will prepare us for the future and plan our course. If we do get off track, remembering our vision will help us get back on course sooner rather than later. Vision inspired by the Holy Spirit can show us a course of action we should take and supply information to guide, counsel, protect, and position us.

Jesus told His disciples that He didn't do anything by Himself, only what He *saw* His Father doing, so He could do the same (John 5:19). Jesus was able to position Himself to see the Father and therefore stay on course to fulfill the Father's vision.

3. Presence

Some individuals receive divine visions and dreams that cause them to experience the presence of God and accept Jesus Christ. I have heard several accounts of Muslims receiving Jesus into their hearts through dreams and visions of Him. Dudley Woodberry, a senior professor of Islamic Studies at the Fuller Theological Seminary, conducted a study in 2007. The study interviewed 750 former Muslims who had converted to Christianity. One of the many reasons they gave for their conversions was a dream they believed was from God.[1] *Mission Frontiers* magazine claims that 25 percent of the six hundred Muslim converts they interviewed experienced a dream that led to their conversion.[2] In these instances, a picture was worth a thousand words.

People of many faiths have been arguing and debating over theology for centuries. However, it's much more difficult to debate with someone over an experience they have had. God loves us so much and can speak to us in specific ways that we are most likely to respond to.

Once God has given us a vision, His presence is what will sustain us through the disappointments and delays. Moses told the Lord that if His presence did not go with him, then he did not want to proceed with God's plan (Exodus 33:15). God assured him that His presence would indeed go. Consequently, Moses was able to lead the tribes of Israel through the wilderness to the promised land and fulfill God's vision. Fulfilling our vision requires that we rely on the presence of the Holy Spirit.

Our Almighty God, who created heaven and earth, wants to be in a present, personal relationship with each of us. We are not merely fans He waves at while climbing into a limousine, or numbers on His social media to indicate power and influence. To Him, we are more than a means of power and importance. We are works of art—children He values and loves and cherishes individually. And He wants us to know Him just as much as He knows us!

Since the beginning, God's desire was to dwell and be present among His people in some form. For a period, His presence was a cloud by day and fire by night (Exodus 13:21-22). Later, His presence dwelled in the tabernacle (Exodus 25:8). In the New Testament, we see that God came to earth in human form through the figure of Jesus and lived among His followers. Because the Holy Spirit came to the church body, the Holy Spirit now resides in every believer's heart (2 Timothy 1:14). It's our Father's desire to be present with His children.

4. Passion

A God-inspired vision can ignite us and energize us! When the responsibilities increase, the costs add up, or the support dwindles, our passion and devotion to see the vision fulfilled is what will fuel us. Visions also support our passion and our gifts. As we delight in the Lord and in seeing His vision fulfilled, He will in turn give us the desires of our hearts (Psalm 37:4). The Lord desires that *His joy* be made full in us (John 13:13). One way of accomplishing this is to focus on God's vision for our future.

It's common to hear the phrase "the passion of the Christ" around the Easter holiday. This refers to the final period before Jesus' death on the cross. Scripture reveals that Jesus endured the cross for the *joy* set before Him (Hebrews 12:2). Passion will keep us focused on our vision with affection, devotion, and joy.

5. Perspective

Having a clearly defined vision will help us maintain perspective. As we look at the events of our day-to-day lives through the lens of our divine vision, we will see that today's challenges prepare us for the future. Maintaining an eternal perspective will help us understand the importance of our vision. What we do today counts for eternity.

We all leave legacies after we're gone, and making a difference in God's Kingdom is the perspective that will motivate us to press on to make them positive and fruitful. Having an eternal perspective helps us take our eyes off our lack in the physical and focus on our abundance in the spiritual.

Jesus was able to live His earthly life while keeping a heavenly perspective. He knew that His actions would count for all eternity. This perspective allowed Him to say, *"It is finished!"* (John 19:30 NIV).

6. Power

A person with vision is powerful! They have a mission, a goal, and an agenda. A person with a *God-given* vision also has supernatural strength, even if they are humanly weak, tired, or afraid. With God, the only qualification needed is a "yes" to His vision. God promises that His strength is enough, and that by His power, one succeeds. Vision gives us the power to be consistent and persistent. We receive superhuman help as the Holy Spirit partners with us to move mountains!

Jesus was the most powerful person in Israel, even when He didn't exert that power all the time. Demons, spirits, sicknesses, diseases, torment, and even death obeyed Jesus. Amazingly, that same Spirit of power is available to you and me today! (Romans 8:11)

7. Provision

As we take steps of faith and obedience in clarifying and fulfilling our God-given vision, we can be hopeful and expectant that God will bring the resources, connections, and grace we need to accomplish His will and purpose in our lives. We can be sure that the Father's provision will come at exactly the right time and in the perfect way.

As Jesus fulfilled His earthly mission and vision, His every need along the way was taken care of. We read of the miraculous coins found in the mouth of a fish; the account of feeding thousands with a young boy's leftovers; a donkey supplied for Him to ride into Jerusalem; an empty upper room was made available for His Passover meal; and an empty tomb was provided for His body.

8. Peace

A vision grounds us and gives us peace. It centers and calms us as we focus on it. Dancers can spin in circles and not get dizzy because they mark a focal point as they turn. That focus keeps them from staggering. In the same way, a clear vision from God gives us a supernatural peace that nothing can shake. Knowing we are following God's plan will bring peace to our souls.

Jesus gave us His peace before He ascended into heaven. He told the disciples that His peace was not of the world, and it would prevent them from becoming fearful, intimidated, or unsettled (John 14:27). In a world full of busyness, having the peace of Christ helps still our minds and respond to the prompting of the Holy Spirit.

Having vision can help us picture our future with hope and faith. Vision helps focus our attention on God's plan and purpose for our lives. Maybe you feel left out because you can't remember any significant vision you have gotten from God. Yet you *have* received a clear-cut vision from God, and it is found in His Word! The scriptures contain enough vision for you and me to last a lifetime! Ultimately, our victory in life comes through our relationship with Jesus Christ. Nevertheless, I encourage you to begin to discover and pursue God's unique vision for your life.

---

1. Woodberry, Shubin, and Mark, "Why Muslims Follow Jesus."

2. "Muslims Tell… 'Why I Chose Jesus,'" Mission Frontiers.

Chapter 3

THE SECRETS OF THE SEERS

The Lord has always shared His vision with His people. Many of these were visions in the mind's eye. God communicated with people consistently through such means. The Bible speaks of how believers "saw" things, and then the Lord communicated what the visions meant. In the Old Testament, God used visions to reveal His plan to His people. In the New Testament, visions and dreams provided divine information, identified Jesus, and helped to establish the Church.

Yet we don't hear of quite as many divine visions today, and certainly not with the firm belief in whoever speaks of one that those in the Bible had. The stories of the Bible took place thousands of years ago, and much has changed in society and culture since then. By the time I began broadening my spiritual sight, I wondered how we knew what truly was a *divine* vision—and not something psychological or manipulated.

The biblical usage of the word "vision" refers to pictures or scenes that were perceived with the physical eyes but also those that were perceived within the mind. A divine vision is an image, scene, or message that is more spontaneous in nature. The Holy Spirit is the source of the vision.

In the Old Testament, one of the Hebrew words for "vision" is the noun *hazon* or *chazown,* which denotes a mental sight, dream, revelation, or oracle. It comes from the root verb *haza* or *chaza,* which means "to see mentally, to perceive, to contemplate, to gaze at, or to behold." In the New Testament, the Greek word used for vision is *horama* and means "a sight or a spectacle." It comes from the root verb *orao,* meaning "to see, behold, or perceive."

In the Bible and today, not everyone receives supernatural visions, and that's okay! God's selection and purpose for such gifts are never truly knowable, but we can discover quite a bit by reading about others' experiences and how those who received them responded.

One thing we can be sure of is that God has shared His vision for us all in His Word and in the form of His Son, Jesus.

ABRAHAM

His story is found primarily in Genesis 12–22.

God spoke to Abraham in different ways, yet all of them required that Abraham engage his imagination and spiritual eyesight, therefore activating his faith. Even today, faith requires us to look forward to a better future even when we may not physically see it yet.

Faith is visionary and requires all of us to believe to a certain extent before we can see. This is where the eyes of our imagination come into play. Abraham had to believe in faith for what had not yet been manifested in the natural realm.

First, he had to see (or imagine) the place God was going to give him as an inheritance. He could not yet see the place, so he needed to use his spiritual eyesight. Then, he had to see (or imagine) the future family that God promised he would have with his eyes of faith because he and his wife were well past childbearing age. We read in Genesis 15:5 that God brought Abraham (then still called Abram) outside of his tent to *look* into the night sky and count the stars above. As many stars as he could *see* and count, that's how many descendants God said he would have.

God is creative, and He gave us this visionary gift when He created us like Him. We are called to create with our words and with our hearts, minds, and eyes. Our imagination fuels the visions that God places in our hearts. It is an important skill in fulfilling our God-given purpose. That's because when God gives us a vision of where we are going and what we will do, as He did with Abraham, we also need to see it and partner with it. If we can imagine the vision, then we can fulfill the vision. Our imagination is the soil in which our faith can grow and mature.

ISAIAH

The prophet Isaiah had numerous divine visions, many of those seen by *"spiritual perception,"* as translated in the Amplified Version (Isaiah 1:1). After Isaiah had the visions, he then told the people of Israel what those visions meant by revelation from the Holy Spirit.

Interestingly, the Bible says that the prophetic words Isaiah spoke were words that Isaiah *saw* (Isaiah 2:1).

I've heard of people who literally see words written on or above people's heads as they minister to them, but I don't think this is what Isaiah is referring to. Here, I believe that God's will was being revealed in Isaiah's mind. As he processed and wrote down what he saw, that revelation literally became words for him to speak to the people of Israel!

The Lord also told Isaiah that He was doing a new thing, but Isaiah should *behold it, perceive it,* and give heed to it (Isaiah 43:19). God asks us to wait with expectation to see what He will show us. Like He did through Isaiah, God can reveal Himself to us through our spiritual eyesight, our minds, and our imaginations. God has a distinct way He wants to communicate with each of us individually because He really loves us that much.

JEREMIAH

Many times, when the prophet Jeremiah received words from the Lord, God would ask him what he *saw*, not what he heard (Jeremiah 1:11,13; 24:3). Jeremiah obeyed and described to God what he envisioned. It's fascinating that God can give us words and prophecies through what we see and choose to focus on, not just what we think we are hearing!

When I began to experience spiritual visions, I thought they were just my imagination, but I quickly discovered they were prophetic words from the Lord. When we are nervous or confused about what we see, we can pray like Jeremiah:

"Lord, this is what I see. What are You showing me? Where *should* I be focusing?"

Don't be afraid to ask God to show you new things. As you learn to see things the way God does, you will broaden your spiritual sight. Perception is everything, and as we learn to focus in on God's voice and views, we will receive more insight.

EZEKIEL

At the beginning of the book of Ezekiel, the prophet was thirty years old and living amid captivity. The heavens were opened, and he saw visions of God. In some ways, this is comforting. God brings things about in His own special timing. For Ezekiel, it was when he was thirty years old. For many people, it's much later than that. I have heard it said that Joseph waited thirteen years, Abraham waited twenty-five years, Moses waited forty years, and Jesus waited thirty years to see visions fulfilled.

Despite the adverse conditions, Ezekiel was still able to see visions from God. He was told by an angel to look, to listen, and to set his heart and mind on what he was shown. Then he was to tell what he saw to the people (Ezekiel 40:4). Ezekiel was in a state of physical difficulty and oppression (during captivity), but he was *still* able to hear from God and be used by Him.

Likewise, if you feel stuck in your current circumstances or conditions, it's important to remember that today's events are empowering you for your future. Even though I've spent the last thirty years in the classroom as a teacher, God has been preparing me for what lies ahead. I'd bet He is doing the same with you. If Jesus had to prepare for thirty years for a three-year ministry, how much more preparation do we need?

Like Ezekiel, these journeys take time, but the Holy Spirit can help us recognize all the ways that we are being prepared for our destinies despite our current circumstances.

DANIEL

In the prophet Daniel's time, he was known as the go-to guy for dream interpretation. Many of Daniel's own visions came while he was sleeping or in a state of rest. When Daniel received his visions and dreams, he was persistent and wanted to make sure he saw all that God wanted to show him. The scriptures tell us he looked and kept looking while having visions (Daniel 7:1-10 AMP). What if Daniel had stopped looking after seeing just one thing?

Spiritual visions and dreams can mean several things and include more than one interpretation. Like Daniel, keep looking, whether you feel closure, defeat, or confusion. Like Daniel, our times of rest can be moments the Father is closest. He loves the quality time with Him that happens when we pause and focus on Him for rest. Perhaps the Lord is going to release more visions and dreams in this time as we learn to rest in Him in this busy and stressful world.

HABAKKUK

Even though the prophet Habakkuk was witnessing perverseness, trouble, violence, and strife in the physical world at the time, the Lord suggested that he look at what was taking place in the spiritual world.

Like Habakkuk, when we meet obstacles in our lives, it's important to look for what God is doing, saying, and showing us spiritually. Part of our spiritual language with God is perceiving and partnering with the waves and moves of the Holy Spirit. Habakkuk also said he would *"watch to see"* what God would say within him (Habakkuk 2:1 AMP). The implication here is that God spoke to him through pictures and images.

God told Habakkuk he would not believe the amazing thing God was going to do even if He told him (Habakkuk 1:5). Rather, Habakkuk had to *see* it to believe it. I might not have ever believed the things about Jesus that have been revealed to me unless I had seen them for myself with the eyes of my spirit. It takes a close relationship with God, trust, and a yearning for what He can show us.

JESUS

His earthly life is documented directly in the four gospels: Matthew, Mark, Luke, and John.

Jesus lived a visionary lifestyle, following His Father's plan. Jesus saw and partnered with the Father's vision. Hebrews 12:2 tells us that for the joy that was *"set before Him",* Jesus endured the cross and sat down at the right hand of the throne of God (AMP). For something to be set before someone, it must be seen, recognized, and acknowledged. Jesus was seeing with His spiritual eyes the spiritual ramifications of going to the cross, not the physical events that were coming at Calvary.

Jesus also said that He was only able to do what He *saw* the Father doing (John 5:19). As followers of Christ, we are called to walk and move after the Holy Spirit, not our physical desires.

Our journey as believers is a walk of faith, not physical sight (2 Corinthians 5:7). We can perceive with the eyes of our hearts, minds, and understanding as we activate our faith.

CORNELIUS AND PETER

The story of Cornelius and Peter working together occurs in Acts 10.

In the book of Acts, we see how God used Cornelius and Peter together to establish His plan of including the gentiles (non-Jewish people) into His family. We read in Acts 10:3 that Cornelius *"clearly saw in a vision,"* and later in Acts 10:11 that Peter *"saw the sky opened up"* (AMP). Both visions were accompanied by voices of angels and the Holy Spirit. Not only that—after Peter had the vision, he also went over it in his mind and meditated on it (Acts 10:19).

Sometimes, we need to ask the Holy Spirit directly for an interpretation of a vision. Other times, He will reveal it to us through other people. God is so excited to partner with us to accomplish His will on the earth! God can use multiple people in partnership to fulfill His mission. It's so beautiful to see how the body of believers is intertwined. Part of seeing with our spiritual eyes is to perceive how God is bringing divine connections with others into our lives.

PAUL

Saul's conversion to Paul happens in Acts 9.

In the book of Acts, Saul of Tarsus, a notorious persecutor of Christians, was blinded by the radiance of God in flashes of heavenly light. The men around him could not see the sight. Then the man was physically blinded for three days. At that time, he saw a *vision* of another believer, Ananias, laying his hands on him to restore his physical sight. Once Ananias laid his hands on him, he regained his physical eyesight and received spiritual eyesight and deep understanding, having been baptized and filled with the Holy Spirit. He was later called "Paul" in Acts 13:9.

After that vision, Paul was never the same! He had several more visions later in life. One vision in the night sent him to Macedonia (Acts 16:9-10). In another night vision, God told him to keep preaching in Corinth (Acts 18:9-11). Paul even said that he had visions and revelations of the Lord where he was in the third heaven (2 Corinthians 12:1-6).

God also wants to renew your spiritual eyesight. Your spiritual vision may have become clouded or unclear over time. Perhaps you've closed your eyes to the vision God has for your life. It's never too late to ask God to remove anything that may be blinding you spiritually.

JOHN

Nearly the entire book of Revelation is a series of visions that the Apostle John had while exiled on the island of Patmos. His visions explain in more detail the events that God showed the prophet Daniel earlier. John was *expecting* to see something, for he said, *"After this I **looked,** and behold"* (Revelation 4:1 ESV, emphasis added). Then the angel showed him what would take place in the future.

It takes a lot of courage to expect to see something from God, no matter how close you are with Him or how well you know your Bible. But just as we read Scripture, pray, worship, and seek wisdom, God wants us to look, to expect, and to believe He will communicate. The good news is, the more you look, the more you will see. Jesus told us that the person who has spiritual knowledge will be given more, but for the person who does not, even what he has will be taken away (Matthew 13:12). Perhaps the Lord is asking us to exile ourselves from our comfort zones, to be alone with Him, and perceive what He wants to show and tell us.

The God-given visions and encounters that many biblical characters have had are available for all those who have the Holy Spirit as the result of being born again! Joel said that on the day of Pentecost that in the last days, *all* believers would have visions—and Peter later repeated this prophecy (Joel 2:28; Acts 2:17).

The Holy Spirit is not limited to a select few. He is actively with each of us full-time, ready to show us God's plan and purpose for

our lives. God can communicate with us any way He chooses. As we expect to hear from Him, He will reveal Himself to us.

Jesus Himself spoke to *all* believers when He declared,

> *"You will **see** greater things than this"* (John 1:50 AMP, emphasis added).

Chapter 4

ILLUMINATING THE WAY

I'm not sure why God chose to reveal Himself to me through visions and dreams, but I'm sure glad He did! Perhaps it's because I tend to be too busy to notice details and veer on the side of logical reasoning more than spiritual understanding. Maybe it's the fact that I felt like an "imposter Christian" who was just going through the motions at church and needed a tangible touch from the Lord. Whatever the reason, I hope that sharing these divine visions will inspire and encourage you to begin envisioning God's Word and plan for *your* own life.

Having clear supernatural vision can transform and define our lives by giving us revelation in several key areas of our lives. Again, the eight elements of spiritual vision are: purpose, position, presence, passion, perspective, power, provision, and peace.

The following spiritual visionary experiences reveal what our general **purpose** as Christians can look like. May they also serve to ignite your own super sight as you begin to see with greater clarity your unique purpose as a follower of Jesus.

THE OIL LAMP

One morning, I was lounging on my basement sofa with my feet kicked back and my eyes closed, talking to God. It was early and the birds were chirping. Suddenly, the image of an old-fashioned oil lamp appeared in my mind, the kind on the tables in some restaurants. As I continued to focus on the lamp in my mind, I could see that the lamp was being stored on the top shelf in a cool, dark basement. The glass on the lamp was covered in dust and was empty of any type of burning oil.

Jesus then appeared in the basement wearing an off-white, tunic-style robe. He took the oil lamp and carefully carried it out of the basement, heading upstairs. I decided to follow Him. Once upstairs, I watched Him dust off the lamp with a rag and delicately fill it with some kerosene oil. Soon after, He lit the lamp with a match and placed the lamp on the kitchen windowsill. As I smelled the burning match, I watched the gentle flicker of the lamp's flame as it danced in the window. Then I opened my eyes and pondered what I had just envisioned.

This was a visual representation of the journey of a believer. At first, we are like empty, dusty oil lamps that find ourselves stuck in a dark place. Then, once Jesus finds us, He takes us out of the dingy basement and moves us into the light upstairs. We have been carried from one place to another in the spiritual realm (Colossians 1:13). Before long, we become filled with oil, which is the symbol of the Holy Spirit. After we have been filled with the presence of God, we are ignited, as we now carry the fire of God within.

One of our purposes as Christians is to be a light that helps others see. We can guide people to the truth, pray for them, and bless them. We get to partner with the Father's plan of bringing the light of Jesus into a dark world.

THE VIRGIN RIVER

Several years ago, Scott and I visited the five national parks of Utah. They are referred to as "The Mighty Five," and I highly recommend visiting! I did a lot of research and planning for the trip, and I remember being so excited to see the giant rock formations. For a couple of nights during the trip, we stayed at a beautiful resort right on the edge of Zion National Park. Our suite had a large balcony overlooking Zion Park and its huge red rock formations, as well as the pristine Virgin River. It was one of the most spectacular and peaceful views I have ever seen. I took several photos and videos of the view so I could remember it forever. I could hear the birds chirping in the trees and the water gently flowing along the river as I enjoyed sitting on the Adirondack chair on the balcony with a cup of coffee. I didn't want to leave that spot when it was check-out time!

A few months after returning home from the Utah trip, I found myself back in the exact spot near Zion in a vision. This time, I wasn't on the balcony of the inn with Scott; I was with Jesus. We were sitting cross-legged on the grassy bank of the Virgin River just at the edge of the resort grounds. I could hear the clear water flowing gently and feel the sun shining above my head. I felt incredibly happy and peaceful.

Jesus then said to me, "Look down into the water. For whatever you see in the water will reflect who you really are."

"Interesting," I thought. As I bent down and looked intently into the cool water, it looked so refreshing, I decided to splash my face and eyes. Soon, I could see the reflection of my face in the water. Amazingly, as I continued to peer attentively into the water, the reflection of my face became Jesus' face! As I was looking for myself in the water, I saw Him.

Later, Jesus stood up and started to walk along the riverbank. He was wearing a tunic and sandals, and He was holding a shepherd's staff in His right hand. I asked Him, "Where are we going?"

He responded, "We're going to find more people so they can peer into the river and find their true identity in Me also."

I opened my eyes and the vision ended.

One of our main purposes is to become more like our Creator. I was reminded of 2 Corinthians 3:18, where Paul says that we behold the glory of the Lord with unveiled faces and are transformed into His very own image. It is God's desire for us to be transformed bit by bit, day by day, and piece by piece into His masterpieces.

We are made in God's image. The more we behold Him, the more we will be able to see who we really are. The Holy Spirit is like a river of living water flowing within us.

Interestingly, over the years, the Virgin River has been carving through the stones of Zion National Park to create some of the most unforgettable scenery. This natural erosion by the Virgin River is responsible for creating "The Narrows," one of the most famous hiking trails in Utah, if not the United States. Although the Virgin River is a food and wildlife source, it's also strong enough to carve through rock! That is what the Holy Spirit purposes to do with us. God gives us hearts of flesh to replace our hearts of stone. He says,

> *"A new heart will I give you and a new spirit will I put within you, and I will take away the **stony heart** out of your flesh and give you a **heart of flesh**"* (Ezekiel 36:26 AMPC, emphasis added).

We can allow the Holy Spirit, like a river, to erode the hardness of our hearts and carve a narrow path of goodness for others to see and experience! As we invite others to experience the blessings of the Lord, we are fulfilling God's vision of enlarging His family.

THE TEA COZY AND THE SHEET

Early one morning, as usual, I had my eyes closed and was listening to some instrumental worship music. I was peacefully soaking in the Lord's presence, and before long, I saw Jesus with the eyes of my spirit. As I kept looking at Him, I noticed that He was making something with His hands. Again, I looked and noticed that He was knitting something. I could hear the gentle clicking of knitting needles and noticed some bright, pink wool. Suddenly, Jesus moved and started to knit all around me! Bewildered, I asked the Lord what He was doing and making. He answered, "I'm knitting a tea cozy."

If you're not familiar, it's a knitted hat-type item that covers a tea kettle to keep the freshly boiled water inside warm and "cozy," especially during colder months. Using one of these tea cozies keeps the water inside the pot hotter for longer. The tea cozy that Jesus had been knitting was created to go all around me, not a kettle! I asked Him, "Why are You making a tea cozy to go around me?"

He replied, "To keep you boiling hot, not lukewarm. It's to keep you fiery hot as if you are on fire for Me."

I looked around my body at the tea cozy, I noticed that it was the same bright pink color as the one I remember seeing in my Auntie Joyce's kitchen in Wales. At that instant, I realized we were standing in my aunt's bright and cheery kitchen. Soon we moved outside to my aunt's backyard.

Jesus was outside standing on the lawn shaking out a large, white sheet. It appeared as if He was shaking off all the dirt and dust it had collected. I could see the dust as it flew in the air. Then He neatly folded the sheet and placed it inside on one of my aunt's shelves.

A couple of things stood out to me from this experience. First, hardly anyone likes to drink lukewarm liquid. Most drinks are designed to be enjoyed either very cold or extremely hot. The book of Revelation frowns upon a "lukewarm" Christian (Revelation 3:16). God desires our genuine passion. A fully authentic Christian is confident in their identity, ability, and assignment. As such, they can offer refreshment to the Lord and to those around them. Likewise, in the book of Matthew, Jesus was upset that the fig tree was deceiving because it displayed leaves but produced no fruit (Matthew 21:19).

God's vision for His people is that they would be stirred up, ablaze with love and devotion for Him.

Secondly, there are times when we need to be shaken up, like the sheet. We can get stuck in routines and need an awakening. We can be inattentive or passive regarding God's vision for our lives. God can shake us out of our stupor to get us to move.

Knowing what you are here for and what God has planned for your life is essential to fulfilling your divine assignments. Striving to be a light to others, becoming more like Jesus, and staying authentic are some of the purposes God has envisioned for all His followers. As you refine your supernatural sight, God's unique plan and purpose for your life will come into clearer view.

Chapter 5

IN STEP WITH THE SPIRIT

Wouldn't it be nice to know if we were in the right place, at the right time, doing the right thing for God? Fortunately, we have God's written Word to guide us in many matters. Still, when it comes to the specific plan that the Lord has for us, knowing which way to turn can be challenging. In the maze of life, the Holy Spirit is our compass, and the Word of God is our map. When our paths seem unclear, having spiritual vision will guide us and give us some much-needed direction to ensure we are in the right position at the right time to succeed. The following spiritual visions helped focus my direction and **position** myself toward God's good plan. It's my hope that they help steer your path through the season of life in which you find yourself.

THE STREAM

Recently, I saw in my spirit one of the most beautiful freshwater streams. It was a clear, bright, sunny summer day. Along the banks of the stream, I could smell the tall pine trees and hear the birds chirping. The contrasting colors of the sapphire sky against the leafy green trees were just beautiful. Soon, Jesus, dressed in white, came into view.

He gently took my hand, and we began walking downstream together, water splashing up to our shins. As the water grew deeper, we began to hop along the larger stones in the stream. The water felt ice-cold on my toes, as I began to giggle like a child. Some of the stones we found were easy to walk upon, but others were quite rough on my feet. At times, the water was waist-deep, and other times, it was shallower. One minute, the stream was very calm, then the next minute it was gushing wildly.

I decided to look around and noticed a few other people in the stream. It was no longer just Jesus and me. Some of them were stuck on a rock, crying in despair and paralyzed in fear. Others were trying to swim through the water but were struggling to stay afloat. I could see their arms waving around exasperatedly as they cried for help. I felt so sorry for them, but all I could do was watch. I glanced around even more and noticed that other people weren't going in the same direction as Jesus and I were. They were walking against the flow of the current and having a rough time making progress through the stream. I felt safe because Jesus was guiding me along the stream. I knew He was supporting me and would catch me if I lost my footing. I was so happy to be going in the same direction the Lord was. I wanted to know where we were going, but I couldn't see past the large bend the stream took. The scene ended, and I opened my eyes.

Just as the water in the stream changed depths and currents, our lives go through seasons. Some days, we seem to be making progress, and others, we can barely get out of bed. Some weeks, we hop along without a care in the world, and other weeks, it hurts just to take another step. Regardless of the outward circumstances or situations in which we may find ourselves, if we take Jesus' hand, He will guide us and support us if we fall. He will ensure that we are in the best position to thrive, taking one step at a time toward our vision. We must let the Holy Spirit guide us, trusting that He knows the best way to go.

THE JUNKYARD

One particular morning, I was singing to God during our church's Sunday service. I tend to close my eyes when I sing to the Lord, and this day was no different. In the middle of one of the songs, suddenly I pictured myself at a large scrap metal junkyard on the outskirts of town. I wondered why I was there, but when I realized Jesus was there standing next to me, I felt reassured.

It was a crisp, autumn evening, and the smell of smoke filled the air. I soon observed several other people hanging out at the junkyard. They huddled together in groups, warming their hands by some small fires. I could just barely see their faces by the light of the flickering flames. Breath rose out of their nostrils and mouths as they spoke into the chilly air.

I didn't really enjoy the feel of the place. It was dark, and the smell of smoke was awful. There was barbed-wire fencing around its border. Several heaps of junk cars formed metal hills all around. The people congregating were standing by smaller piles of junk. As I focused on the heaps, I realized they were piles of trash that were burning.

Some people had exceptionally large piles of trash which produced high flames, while others had small piles with just a few embers.

The Lord must have sensed that I was confused. He explained, "The piles of junk the people are burning represent the things they have surrendered to Me. Some have only given Me very few things, and they have smaller piles. Others have given Me many things, and they have larger piles."

I wondered what types of things the people had or hadn't given to Jesus. Again, sensing my question, He continued: "The people who have the largest fires are the ones who have surrendered many aspects of their lives to Me."

I looked again at those with large heaps and high flames and marveled at them. All at once, I realized that I too was standing by my own burning pile of junk. I peered down at my own pile and saw that it was medium sized. It wasn't as small as some, but it wasn't nearly the size of others. I felt such a longing to surrender more things in my life to God that I was still holding on to. The worship song ended, and I opened my eyes.

Following God's vision can be frightening. What may appear to be a dark, dismal place may be where the Holy Spirit is leading us to find light and clarity. What I thought was an unnerving, depressing location was really a place of freedom and surrender. **God can prepare us by positioning us!**

THE BRICKS

Another Sunday morning during praise and worship at church, I had a further encounter. Jesus appeared again in my mind's eye. This time, He was wearing off-white overalls like painters wear. He wasn't painting but kneeling as He built a brick wall. It was a steamy, muggy day, and He was a bit sweaty! The Lord was working very meticulously as He laid one red brick upon another. I could hear his trowel scraping the mortar onto the bricks.

Jesus was on one side of the waist-high wall, and I was on the other side. Then I realized that I had a brick in my hand. I felt like I was supposed to hand the brick to Him. So I did. As soon as I handed the brick to Jesus, He explained to me that He uses the pieces of ourselves (the bricks) as building materials for houses in heaven for His family. As the song ended, so did the vision.

In the Old Testament, bricks represented slavery and bondage, referring to a time when the Israelites were forced into labor by having to make bricks day after day for the Egyptians. Today, we are the house (or temple) of the Holy Spirit. We are a human home where God chooses to live. With God as our Carpenter, we can become masterpieces of His goodness. We position ourselves to be a vessel for Him to fill and use. As we offer God things such as our time, affection, and resources, He takes those things and constructs them into something new and beautiful.

Arriving at our destination without a clear roadmap to follow can be daunting. Still, faith requires that we trust the Holy Spirit's leadership. Sometimes it may seem as if we have taken a wrong turn, or we've ended up in the wrong place. Yet God may be positioning us for promotion. As we humble ourselves, God will elevate us. We are promised that as we submit to God, He will direct our steps (Proverbs 3:6). Our ultimate destination is our heavenly home, lovingly constructed by God in our hearts, but we can continue to refine our Kingdom vision while here on the earth.

What can you learn from a place or position you're currently in? How might God be using that situation to prepare you for greater things in the future? Which areas of your life might you be trying to steer that the Holy Spirit would like to lead?

Chapter 6

DIVINE INDWELLING

Moses partnered with God's vision of delivering Israel. As such, Yahweh promised that His *presence* would be with him. When his successor, Joshua, arrived at the promised land, God again promised that His *presence* would be with him wherever he went (Joshua 1:9).

In the book of Daniel, Shadrach, Meshach, and Abednego refused to worship the king's gods. As such, when they were thrown into a furnace as a result, a fourth man's *presence* appeared in the furnace, like the son of the gods (Daniel 3).

When Jesus gave His followers what we refer to as the "Great Commission" (of making disciples of all nations), He promised to be with them until the end of the age (Matthew 28:20).

There is a direct correlation between God's plan and God's **presence**. Participating and partnering with the Lord and His vision means He will be by our side. Feeling closer to God and sensing the leading of the Holy Spirit is a byproduct of pursuing our divine assignments in faith.

THE CASTLE

My mother is Welsh, so I grew up off and on in the small country of Wales. As a child, my Nana would often take me for a walk to Oystermouth Castle and its lush grounds. The castle dates from the twelfth century and sits atop a forty-foot-high limestone ridge overlooking the village of Mumbles. I used to run and play there for hours, pretending to be a princess of an ancient land. One morning in my adulthood, during my quiet time with the Lord, I was concerned for my Welsh family, ancestors, and the whole country. Other than hearing about the Welsh Revival in the early 1900s, it seemed as if Wales had forgotten God.

As I closed my eyes to pray about the situation, I immediately pictured Jesus and myself sitting on one of the park benches of the castle grounds, exactly where my Nana and I used to sit. It was a bright sunny day, and the sound of children playing filled the air. Some people were walking their dogs, others were jogging; it was a typical summer day in a seaside village. Soon I realized that Jesus and I were eating fish and chips from the local "chippie" at the bottom of the hill.

Jesus was seated to my right. From this viewpoint, high above, we could see the bay and the entire village below. I had often taken photographs from that very spot. As we opened our bags of chips, I asked Jesus if He wanted any salt for His chips. He looked right at me, grinned, and said, "Yes, salt is good!" We chuckled about that for a few moments because I knew it was a reference to His words in the Gospel of Mark.

Then, perceiving what was on my heart that morning, Jesus reminded me of what was written in Scripture, in Psalm 2:8, about how God gives us the nations if we ask, and that included Wales. Then, Jesus prompted me to say a prayer aloud with Him for Wales. I obliged and prayed with Jesus for few minutes. He listened very intently while I prayed and nodded in agreement. I opened my eyes after the prayer ended and felt real peace after the encounter.

God's sweet presence on the bench as I prayed for my Welsh family meant a great deal. I wonder how many times we have prayed and wondered if anyone was listening. Rest assured, if we are praying God's will and vision, His presence is with us. If the idea of hanging out on a park bench and eating fries with someone as holy and important as Jesus seems crazy or intimidating, ask Him to reveal to you the ways He wants to be in your presence—and in ways that are meaningful to you. **Remember, Christianity is a *relationship with Christ*, not just a religion.**

THE SPINNING ONE

One day at church, I was watching a young woman as she knelt on the floor in front of the altar. She was deep in worship with her eyes closed and her hands raised as she praised the Lord. There were four small children dancing close by her. After a little while, the oldest child began to run in circles around the woman kneeling. Soon after, the other three children began to follow suit and run around the young woman. As I witnessed the scene unfold with my physical eyes, I began to see another scene simultaneously with my spiritual eyes.

The church band was singing, "From you are all things, and to you are all things, you deserve the glory!"

At that instant, I saw the planets in the sky that God had created. I saw the sun, the earth, and the moon. They were all spinning on their axis, rotating in perfect harmony and order.

Then the Lord said, "The heavenly bodies spin because *I* spin."

A few moments later, I gently heard the Lord say to me, "I love to dance and encircle you. I spin around you and delight in you!"

Instantly, I recalled the words of the prophet Zephaniah, who said that the Lord is in our midst and that He rejoices over us with singing (Zephaniah 3:17). The root of the Hebrew word for "rejoice" in that verse is *gheel*, which means "to *spin around* with violent emotion," or "to dance with joy." God is not just presently in our midst; He is also singing and spinning around us because He delights to be with us!

I glanced back at the children. They were still jumping and dancing around the woman, delighting in the moment. The innocence of the children's smiles coupled with the authenticity of the woman's worship were just heavenly.

The Lord's presence is always with us. As New Testament believers, the Holy Spirit has come to live and remain on the inside of each one of us. We might know this on an intellectual level, but understanding that on a personal, meaningful level can be a bit more challenging. Nevertheless, as we pray and worship the Lord, He *is* present, even if we can't feel or see it. As we learn to envision His presence with our eyes of faith, we will increasingly encounter Him. When do you seem to sense God's presence the most? How can you increase those types of experiences into your schedule?

Chapter 7

PURE PASSION

The word "passion" is used to describe a powerful or compelling emotion or feeling. In most cases, it refers to a feeling of love or intense desire. When the Bible refers to the "passion of the Christ," it refers to the painful death that Jesus suffered on our behalf in fulfilling the Father's vision of our salvation and redemption. God has such great love for us that He gave us His Son so that anyone who believes in Him will have eternal life (John 3:16).

Love comes from God Himself, and *His* love has been placed in our hearts by the Holy Spirit (Romans 5:5; 1 John 4:7). **That's a fascinating idea: the One who created love has deposited that same love into His creation.**

I used to ponder scriptures about loving others and felt defeated, thinking I had better muster up some more love for the people around me. Let's face it, loving a harsh boss, a meddling neighbor, an erratic driver, or a cynical relative can be challenging. However, it's not about sensing more of *our* love for others; it's about allowing *God's* love to shine more brightly through us.

A visionary lifestyle inspired by the Holy Spirit will bring energy and passion into our day-to-day lives. People can endure many hardships along the way if they are passionate about something or someone. **Passion** gives us much-needed strength to continue pursuing our visions. Envisioning a future we are passionate about will increase our hope and joy levels today.

THE DANCE

One time, I envisioned myself in the ballroom where my husband and I had our wedding reception. The room was dimly lit, and candles gently flickered. The fire was brightly burning in the stone fireplace, and thick green velvet curtains covered the windows, making the room warm and inviting even though it was a cold, winter evening.

As the jazz band played softly on stage, several well-dressed couples slow-danced to the music on the dance floor. I looked down at myself and realized I was wearing a white wedding dress. I was dancing cheek-to-cheek with the Lord! He held me so close I could even feel His heartbeat and breath on my cheek and in my ear. We swayed to the music and enjoyed a sweet embrace of heavenly love and affection. I looked down at the parquet wood floor and saw Jesus' shiny black shoes. As my eyes rose, I saw that Jesus wore a black suit and tie. I perceived He was the bridegroom, and I was His bride.

As we danced, the other couples watched the two of us. Yet Jesus made me feel as if I was the only person in the room. As we moved, I felt more love, acceptance, and safety than I ever had before. As the jazz band ended the song, so did the encounter.

THE VEIL

Yet another time, I saw with my spiritual eyes an old white church—the kind you may find in the country. The original dark oak pews were empty of parishioners. There was complete silence and stillness in the chapel. Soon I discovered I was walking down the red-carpeted aisle dressed as a bride. I wore a traditional white lace dress along with a veil over my face. I looked up ahead at the altar and saw Jesus eagerly waiting for me to approach Him. He was dressed as the groom in a black suit and tie with a crisp white shirt underneath. He wore a single daffodil in His lapel. (The daffodil is the national flower of Wales, by the way). I proceeded to walk down the aisle to meet this handsome Prince of Peace. When I reached Jesus, He stretched His arms and carefully lifted the wedding veil that was covering my face. As He did, He didn't verbally speak, but His eyes spoke to me saying, "The veil has been lifted. You can see Me as I really am, and I can see you for who you really are." I must have opened my eyes, and the encounter ended.

There is nothing we need to hide from the One who created us, loves us, and died for us, and there is nothing hidden by God the Father from us, for it has all been revealed in His Son. Both related visions evoked feelings of complete love, acceptance, and undiminished passion from the Lord. I imagine it's easier for a woman to relate to the idea of the Church being the bride of Christ than a man (Ephesians 5:25-27). Still, we are all children whom God loves tenderly and passionately. The idea of a bride and groom parallels the close relationship we have with our Savior. It is the concept of two becoming one, as we become one with Christ. This idea also reveals God's faithfulness and commitment to His union with His children.

THE CROSS

Nothing exemplifies passionate love more than Jesus' death and sacrifice for us on the cross. I have envisioned the cross in my mind's eye on several occasions. One encounter, however, gave me a viewpoint I had not seen before.

I was a bystander in the crowd at Calvary as Jesus Christ was hanging on the cross. He hung in the middle while two other criminals were to His left and right. A strange dark haze hovered in the sky. I could hear crows flying above and a few women crying below. Some of the onlookers watched attentively at what was happening while others were just nosey, trying to see what the commotion was. I felt as if I was stuck in time, somehow warped into a specific period in eternity. After taking in the crowd, I decided to glance up at Jesus' face. He instantly made eye contact with me—as if to say, "I see you. This is for you." His swollen and watery eyes were like liquid ink. I melted inside.

Soon, I noticed two papyrus-type pages nailed on both the left and right sides of the cross. Both papers had handwriting on them. I continued to look and could see that the paper on the left had a list of all the commandments from the Old Testament that I had broken! The paper on the right had a list of all the sicknesses and diseases I had ever had!

"What in the world?" I thought to myself. I wondered if anyone else was able to read the pages, hoping they were only visible to me. While I was still concerned about the pages being read, suddenly, some of Jesus' burgundy-colored blood dripped onto both pages. Then a few more drops of blood fell. As the drops fell, they began to blot out the pages until both were illegible. Neither note could be read any longer; all that remained were two blood-stained pages.

As I awoke from the vision, I felt such gratitude for what Christ accomplished on the cross not only for me but for all of us. The Greek word *sozo* means to be saved, delivered, preserved, protected, healed, and made whole by the blood of Jesus. Through Christ's passionate sacrifice on the cross, we have been *sozo*-ed. This was God's love on display.

As we earnestly desire to see more with our spiritual eyes and pursue our divine vision with passion, the Holy Spirit's love (in us) will eliminate fear and insecurity. This allows us to continue moving forward toward our heavenly goal.

Are there things in your life that you've been doing without passion or purpose? We are encouraged to do *all* things as if we were doing them for the Lord instead of for people (Colossians 3:23-24). One way of finding more joy and passion in our lives is by giving more of ourselves and the light that we carry away. The parts of our lives that passion touches, Jesus' presence and fullness appear.

Can you envision yourself being completely loved, forgiven, accepted, and healed by God today? How can you receive more of God's love now? In what meaningful ways can you put God's love into action?

Chapter 8

THE VIEW FROM ABOVE

I've heard it said that "perspective is everything"—meaning that how we perceive and interpret our environments, circumstances, and relationships affects how we feel and act. We can be glass-half-full people or glass-half-empty people. As believers, we have the privilege of gaining a heavenly **perspective** rather than just keeping an earthly one. King Solomon, for example—though rich, powerful, and full of wisdom—wrote this toward the end of his life:

> *"I have seen all the things that are done under the sun;*
> *all of them are meaningless, a chasing after the wind."*
> (Ecclesiastes 1:14 NIV)

Even as the anointed king and the son of the great psalmist King David, Solomon struggled. As he grew older, he maintained an earth-bound viewpoint as opposed to keeping a heavenly perspective. The phrase "under the sun" is repeated throughout the book of Ecclesiastes and refers to earthly endeavors apart from God. Looking at life only from the earth's angle resulted in Solomon's sorrow over meaningless activities and ambitions. His earthly point of view was limited. Wisdom, work, power, wealth, and life itself are pointless *without* God.

The Apostle James, on the other hand, urged believers to be joyful when trouble came. He had a heavenly perspective. He knew that the trials of life brought strength, perseverance, and maturity to continue following Jesus (James 1:2-4). There is a reward awaiting those who persevere in hope. Life *with* God is full of purpose and meaning.

Pursuing a God-given vision will allow us to see things in a different light. We will realize that problems can be opportunities, and today's trials can teach and equip us for tomorrow. Accurately viewing God, ourselves, our circumstances, and other people is vital to living a victorious life in Christ and to start seeing those mountains move! The following encounters demonstrate the higher viewpoint from which we can see our lives.

THE TEAPOTS

I've been an avid tea drinker my whole life, so it was no surprise to me one Sunday morning when I envisioned my favorite beverage. I was singing at church with my eyes closed when suddenly everyone in the sanctuary turned into small white teapots. The people, now teapots, were filled with steaming-hot water. As teapots do, they had tea bags soaking in them. As the tea bags were seeping into the hot water, the water became infused with the flavor of the tea. Then the hot tea (from inside the people) was poured into several small, white teacups.

Jesus then appeared as the waiter. He was wearing the traditional black-and-white waiter uniform, complete with a bow tie and vest. He began to carry all the teacups on a silver tray and passed out the filled teacups for the others seated at tables to enjoy. The worship ended, and I opened my eyes.

As followers of Jesus, we're a bit like tea pots filled with hot water. Just as tea bags steep in water, so the Holy Spirit steeps in our souls. Like tea in water, we can extract the flavor of the Holy Spirit in our hearts. The Spirit fills us with His presence, but not so that we can just enjoy a cup of Him, but so that the Holy Spirit can be poured out and shared with others.

Having a higher, heavenly perspective allows us to realize that life's not just all about us. As followers of Jesus, we strive to live unselfish lives in love and to help and encourage others. **Once we realize that our giftings and talents have been given to us for the benefit of others, we will begin to make a positive impact on the world for God's Kingdom.**

THE FENCE

Another Sunday morning during worship at church, I had a vision where I saw Jesus with my spiritual eyes. I saw Him slowly walk up and down the aisles of our church. He was wearing His typical off-white, one-piece tunic and sandals, and His hair flowed freely as He strolled by. He was smiling and humming to the music. I was happy to see Him among us. The others in the room didn't seem to see Him or appear distracted as they continued to sing.

Jesus kept moving around the sanctuary and gently placed His right hand on each person's head as if to bless them. As I continued to watch the Lord interact with the church members, some of them transformed into columns of fire! It was as if their human shapes disappeared, and the only thing left was a body-sized flame. Nothing else in the church was burning or smoking and the burning ones didn't seem to sense anything happening to them. As Jesus continued to move about, some other people turned into human-sized pieces of molten metal. Some even had embers begin to spark out of them! Several more of the crowd's bodies became filled with this red-hot iron. After that, the glowing hot bodies twisted themselves together to form an intricate, wrought-iron fence!

I realized that I was also one of the glowing ones and was also a part of the iron fence. It was as if we were being forged together, as we bent and curled until we became a complete, ornate fence. What a worship set that was!

Interestingly, wrought iron is a soft iron with high elasticity, so it can be heated and reheated, and worked into various shapes. The word "wrought" means to be worked into shape by artistry or effort or processed for use. Similarly, God can remold and recreate us for good works. Our works are therefore wrought with God, meaning they are divinely prompted and completed (John 3:21).

Keeping God's perspective of others causes us to see the value in them. No one makes a fence out of a single piece of metal. As we pursue a God-given vision, many times, we will need to collaborate with other individuals. Seeing others from a higher viewpoint helps us see them as integral parts of God's overall vision. This will help us recognize and value the significance of others.

As believers, we all have access to God's grace, ability, and power to participate in His plan. Maintaining the perspective that *everyone,* including you and me, has divine tasks will help us clarify our vision and help those around us focus on theirs.

SEATED IN HEAVEN

One of the first times I had what I would call a spiritual vision, my eyes were closed, and I began to see a movie-like scene in my mind. To my surprise, I saw myself in heaven. I was holding Jesus' hand as we flew through the air like Supermen in heaven. Yes, flying! Spiritual eyesight sees beyond what our physical eyes can understand.

Oddly, I wasn't afraid of heights anymore. Jesus began to give me a brief tour of the supernatural place. The colors were amplified, as if I was looking at everything through a vibrant filter. Forms and shapes were crisp and clear, like when I first wore a pair of polarized prescription sunglasses. I recognized several of the people there, but there were many that I didn't know.

Soon we stopped flying, and Jesus stood by my side. I felt at peace, but I must have been crying because the Lord began to wipe away the tears that had been falling down my face. He tousled my hair and placed a beautiful silver crown sparkling with diamonds on top of my head. Up to this point, Jesus hadn't spoken, but we had been able to communicate in our spirits without needing words.

Then He said, "You are a daughter of the King and therefore a princess!"

Amazingly, Jesus took His mouth and breathed into my mouth. He said, "Receive the Holy Spirit!" Just as He did with His disciples in the book of John. He told me to remember this heavenly realm and perspective of *who* I was and *where* I was. I opened my eyes and quickly wrote down all I could remember from the encounter.

Is there a way for us to remember we are spiritually seated in heaven while simultaneously existing here on the earth? It's not easy, but it is possible to maintain a heavenly perspective as we go through our daily living. What should our heavenly perspective be? Envisioning ourselves as seated above will help us work from a place or rest as we trust in Jesus' finished work, which gives us blessing and victory. Recognizing the authority we hold as God's children will encourage us to move forward should difficulties arise. Believing the Holy Spirit's power is working in us will help us live in peace and joy.

Since the majority of our lives will be spent in eternity, we would be wise to keep a heavenly perspective regarding our earthly decisions. As we view our ordinary lives through a supernatural lens, we will more easily find our divine assignments, our kingdom connections, and the victory that is ours in Christ Jesus. We can learn to look through the lens of God's truth and love to see the overall picture and higher purpose of our lives here and now. How can you begin to see more clearly with the vision from heaven instead of the clouds of doubt from the earth?

Chapter 9

EMPOWERED FOR MORE

The Holy Spirit empowers believers by giving them grace. Grace is a popular word in Christian circles, but what exactly is it? Grace is God's supernatural enablement that allows us to accomplish what we never could on our own. It is the favor of God.

Grace is an undeserved gift from God that gives us extraordinary favor, ability, resources, and power to accomplish God's will and develop His character in our lives. Grace is God's power that assists us in carrying out His purpose beyond our human ability. The Holy Spirit's power can empower us to face our fears, conquer challenges, and remain firm in faith. The Holy Spirit also gives us specific giftings and qualities we can learn to develop. Visualizing the power of the Holy Spirit working in us gives us the confidence and the ability to live a life that thrives. These amazing visions authenticate the supernatural **power** that God has given us to accomplish what He asks of us.

THE CROWN

Another Sunday morning at church, as we were singing a song to King Jesus, I closed my eyes and my spiritual eyes opened.

Immediately I saw Jesus with a crown on His head. It wasn't the crown of thorns, but a royal crown designed and preserved for a king. It was large, golden, and shining. Various jewels were embedded in the crown, making it sparkle like a rainbow. It was glorious! Then, as I heard the church members continue to sing, they also appeared in the vision, and we all lifted our faces in adoration to the Lord.

Amazingly, Jesus bowed His chin in acknowledgment as we praised Him. Suddenly, His golden crown began to liquefy. The crown began to drip liquid gold droplets that showered our heads, faces, and shoulders! Then King Jesus began to laugh and shake His head, as if to make even more drops of the liquid gold fall on us! I opened my eyes to peer at the crowd. They seemed mesmerized as they raised their hands in adoration of their King. We were all covered in God's beauty, splendor, and radiance (His glory) in the spiritual realm.

There are several references to crowns in Scripture. A crown can symbolize the blessing of children, old age, and of wisdom (Proverbs 4:9; 16:31; 17:6). We can also expect an imperishable crown that awaits us in heaven (1 Corinthians 9:25). The Lord loves to share all that He has with us, including His glory and His power. Father God is happy to give us the Kingdom and encourages us to reign in life through the grace of Jesus (Luke 12:32; Romans 5:17).

THE SHEPHERD

On another occasion, I was spending quiet time with the Lord when I envisioned Jesus again. We were outside in a large, open field. He stood in front of me dressed as a shepherd. He wore a light-colored robe and held a tall, wooden shepherd staff in His hand. I saw the scars (from the cross) on His hands as He held His staff. As I beheld Jesus in complete adoration, He gently reached over to me and took off a tight headband that I was apparently wearing. Amazingly, after Jesus took the headband off my head, He put it on His own head! Once the headband was on Jesus' head, it turned into a crown of thorns.

I looked in wonder at what Jesus had just done but was too mesmerized to ask Him any questions. Next, I saw some beams of light come out of the scars in His hands. It was as if there were beams of sunshine streaming out of His hands. Then, Jesus took both of my hands and held them in His. Immediately, I felt intense heat inside of my hands as the light beams penetrated my skin. He held them for a long time and stared silently into my eyes.

After an intense minute, Jesus said, "Your hands *are healed* and are *for healing.*"

The encounter ended, and I thanked God for such a beautiful picture. You see, God has a good plan of restoration and abundance for all of us. Perhaps you're thinking, "Well if that's the case, then why am I not seeing it in my life?" That's a valid question that I honestly can't answer. I do know what God has promised us in His Word, and I am confident that we will one day see God's goodness working in us and for us. Having a specific vision from God can be a powerful reminder of what is possible if we believe. If I'm ever tempted to wallow in headache pain or arthritic hand pain, I remember what God has done and spoken.

Perhaps the Holy Spirit is prompting you to visualize the power that is available to you. As you begin to see with your eyes of faith, this supernatural grace and ability will enable you to proceed in power. We have been empowered through our union with Jesus Christ. **As we draw our strength from Him, we become supernaturally infused with His strength (Ephesians 3:20; 6:10).**

THE DRESS

Sometimes dreams are silly ways our brains process life, but occasionally they can have a profound impact. I don't often have divinely inspired dreams, but one night I dreamed about an expensive and exquisite dress. This dress was handmade and meticulously woven together using honeybee wings, of all things! As such, it was very delicate and fragile. The shimmer of the bee wings gave the dress a golden chiffon appearance. In the dream, I was the one who was wearing the dress, but everyone else wanted the dress. I felt like a movie star at the Oscars, with cameras snapping at every angle to get a photo. However, there were some "bad guys" trying to steal the dress like in a James Bond film. The dress went missing at some point in the dream, but my team of "good guys" were able to retrieve it, so I was able to wear it again.

I awoke that morning from the dream and thought I heard someone speaking, but I looked over at my husband and he was still sleeping.

I then heard the following words in my spirit: "It's the *anointing*!"

I asked, "What's the *anointing*?"

I sensed that God was telling me that the dress in the dream was a symbol of the anointing. The golden, honey-toned, lacey bee wings were God's glory, and His anointing was adorning me. Biblically speaking, when someone was anointed, they would have aromatic oil rubbed on their heads as part of a ceremony to show divine approval and appointment. Many kings in the Bible were anointed, and some still are in certain countries.

In modern-day Christianity, the anointing signifies God's favor, ability, and power upon someone. Christ, which translates as "the anointed one," lives inside of us. Therefore, we have all been anointed by God if we believe in Jesus the Anointed One (1 John 2:20). We tend to think only special pastors or evangelists are anointed, but that simply isn't true. Satan, our enemy— portrayed as the bad guys in the dream—wants us to believe the lie that we don't have God's favor, ability, or power. He wants to stifle our effectiveness through fear and unbelief.

As we learn to move from a performance-based mindset and embrace the grace and power that has already been imparted to us, we will be able to partner with the Holy Spirit's leading to fulfill God's vision for our lives. God's presence empowers us to move mountains and push back the darkness we see.

Which tasks in your life do you feel unqualified to tackle? How can you allow God's power to work through you despite any weakness you may feel? What could you accomplish if you believed you were well-equipped and able?

Chapter 10

ENVISION THE PROVISION

We've discussed the idea that we are already powerful and anointed because the Holy Spirit lives inside of us. I would also like to propose that everything else we need to pursue and fulfill our God-given vision and mission will be provided for us. As the Israelites pursued the promised land, they were given miraculous food from heaven for each day. When they later became thirsty in the desert, God supplied water out of a rock for them to drink (Exodus 16-17).

We can respond to the Holy Spirit's leading (perhaps by an inner prompting or voice, or by a particular sense or feeling) and take one step of faith at a time. As we take that step forward, our divine **provision** comes. God loves to provide for us in response to our faith, prayers, and praise. The waters of the Red Sea didn't begin to part until *after* the people moved (at God's command) and Moses stretched out his hand (Exodus 14:15-22). The walls of Jericho didn't fall until *after* the army marched around them for seven days (Joshua 6). Jesus Himself assured us that as we seek His Kingdom and righteousness (His way of life), everything we need will be provided. In this world, people have to find their own provision, but as God's children, our Father knows what we need and will faithfully supply (Matthew 6:31-33). The subsequent dreams and visions confirm that God will meet our needs abundantly!

CHOPPED

Scott and I had been transitioning from one church to another. We had been in a very dry season and were looking for more ministry opportunities. Around this time, our church had decided to start a "Healing Room" ministry once a month. Scott was excited to be a part of the new ministry from the get-go, but I was a bit apprehensive. I began to devour teaching materials on how to pray for others. I listened to podcasts and CDs, read books, and took notes in preparation for this new ministry. During this time, I had the following dream.

In this dream, I was on a cooking show similar to the one called *Chopped*. If you've never seen it, let me briefly explain. Four contestants are given a certain number and amount of specific ingredients and a set amount of time to create either an appetizer, entrée, or dessert for three judges to taste. There are about five food items, given in a basket, that *must* be included in the preparation of the dish. There are also refrigerated and pantry items for the contestants to use (or not use) as they wish. The kitchen is full of appliances and gadgets, so the contestants are free to prepare, cook, and serve the food as they desire. Once the time is up, their dishes are tasted and critiqued by three judges who are usually chefs and restaurateurs. After each round, one contestant is "chopped" from the competition, which means they are sent home.

There I was, one of the contestants on this cooking show in my dream! I was in a real panic, searching for a specific ingredient I wanted to include in my dish. I was running behind the other contestants because I was spending too much time looking for one ingredient in the pantry. Consequently, when the buzzer sounded and time was up, I made little to no progress on my dish; I had spent all my time searching for one ingredient. Afterward, I realized that I had been looking in the pantry for a specific ingredient that was already in the basket the whole time! Each ingredient I was looking for had already been provided. All I had to do was use them to prepare the dish. Needless to say, I did not win the round or the show and got "chopped."

As I processed the dream the next day, I felt that the Lord was telling me through the dream that everything I need for ministry He has already provided. The Holy Spirit has already provided superabundant grace and gifts to all of us.

Therefore, if we want to begin serving in new ways in our church or community, we don't need to be afraid or insecure, thinking that we don't have what we need. We don't need to look for any special anointing, gifting, or strategy to pray for others as if we are searching for a key ingredient to a recipe. Rather, we just need to access the spiritual basket of provision that is already on the table in front of us.

THE SPIRAL CLOUDS

Sometimes our dreams can contain supernatural answers to problems or concerns we may have in the natural realm. One July, I was enjoying my summer off as a teacher, but like most teachers, I was thinking about the upcoming school year in the fall. Soon after, I had a dream wherein the clouds in the sky were unlike any clouds I had ever seen. They were spiral, curly-Q clouds. These clouds were rotating and spinning vertically instead of horizontally. I was a bit startled but also curious when I awoke from the dream.

I had no idea what the clouds symbolized, but I drew the clouds and wrote about the dream in my journal. As I studied the dream, I wondered if it was some sort of forecast of a tornado or hurricane. Perhaps God was putting things into motion in the heavens.

A month or so later, I was back in school, attending a meeting with my fellow teachers. Suddenly, one of my colleagues had the brilliant idea of recycling and rotating certain content for some of our classes. The other teachers and I were overjoyed at the thought and quickly put a plan into motion that saved a great deal of our time and energy, benefiting the students greatly.

Later that school year, during my quiet time with the Lord, I was prompted to go back and read some of my previous journal entries. As I was flipping through the pages, I came across my drawing of the clouds, and realized that the Lord had been trying to tell me what to do in that situation back in July! He had already shown me the rotating, cyclical, recycling clouds in that dream.

Our Father is more than willing to help solve our problems and provide us with wisdom if we simply ask Him. The Holy Spirit, who is the Counselor, is ready and willing to counsel you in the affairs of your life. Allow Him to guide you and speak to you in numerous ways, including dreams.

SPRING CLEANING

One morning, I was alone in the house, and the Lord appeared to me in my mind's eye in front of the fireplace in the living room. He was carrying a large, brown moving box.

He said, "It's time to move things around and clean things up!"

Then I watched as He continued to carry several boxes out of the house. As I looked a little closer, I could see that the boxes were labeled. Normally when people clear things out or move, they label boxes with things such as "dishes" or "clothes," but in this vision, the boxes were not labeled as such. These boxes were labeled with the words: "fear," "pride," "worry," "anger," and "disappointment." I asked the Lord what He meant by all this.

He answered, "Julia, I want to bring new things into your life, so I am making room for those new things by removing the old ones."

As I continued to watch Jesus go out of the front door and load the boxes into a truck, I saw Him come back in the front door with some new items. First, He brought in a vibrant, green plant. Then, He brought in a small, decorative water fountain. Later, He brought in a scruffy but happy black-and-white dog. Everything that the Lord brought into the house was full of life, and everything He took out was void of the Holy Spirit, ineffective or unnecessary. I was amazed that the *Lord* was doing this, not me. I was simply resting in His grace and goodness as He was improving the surroundings. As I opened my eyes after the vision, I felt invigorated and excited about the new things God was going to bring about in my life.

God has new things He wants to do in all of our lives. Invariably that may require a spiritual spring cleaning. As we allow the Holy Spirit to fill and occupy more parts of our hearts and minds, we open the door to the provision and supply from heaven. God is our Source. Our resources may change along the way, but our Source never does. Moving forward with our eyes of faith is not an easy task, but then again, no one ever said following Jesus would be easy.

Asking, acknowledging, and thanking God for His divine provision *before* seeing any evidence of His supply is how it will appear.

Perhaps you're looking for innovative ideas and strategies at work or in your business. Maybe you need wisdom to make a major decision. You might be searching for the right opportunity or connection to move forward. Whatever it is, God is fully aware and fully able to meet your needs abundantly in His divine provision.

Chapter 11

PEACE FROM ANOTHER PLACE

In today's hyper-busy world, learning how to find and maintain peace can be challenging, but it is necessary. The biblical word for **peace** (*shalom*) has a much broader meaning than the English equivalent. The biblical concept of peace encompasses completeness, safety, health, prosperity, tranquility, contentment, and undisturbed well-being. It signifies a state of nothing missing, needed, or even wanted because everything is safe, sound, complete, and whole. That sounds wonderful, doesn't it?

While we may never be able to attain this total concept of peace on this side of heaven, we will find more peace as we follow God's Word, will, and vision for our lives. Visualizing the peace that is available to us through Christ can also bring us relaxation, relief, and rest. As we search for more contentment and satisfaction in life, let these visions of peace inspire you today.

THE PICNIC

My husband and I enjoy getting away and staying at picturesque bed-and-breakfasts from time to time. One day, I was resting on the couch in our basement with my eyes closed. Suddenly Jesus appeared in my mind's eye. I glanced around and noticed that we were at a bed-and-breakfast Scott and I had visited several years ago. This inn had a lot of land, so the innkeepers made several trails and pathways throughout the grounds for guests to enjoy. One of the trails meandered through tall grass, up a hill, and into a large, open meadow full of wildflowers. Butterflies and birds hovered over the flowers as large, puffy clouds filtered the summer sunshine. The smell of the wildflowers and the grass added to the serene scene.

As I looked around some more, Jesus was sitting on a soft, baby blue blanket. He was wearing a shorter off-white tunic with short sleeves. He had prepared a picnic lunch and was waiting for me to join Him. Of course, I obliged. We enjoyed some cheese, crackers, salami, fruit, pastries, and other goodies, as well as some sparkling pink lemonade. We laughed, joked, and shared ideas. Afterward, we rested on the grass as our food settled. We gazed up at the puffy clouds and the baby blue sky, feeling the breeze on our faces. The vision ended as I opened my eyes.

The modern-day concept of a bed-and-breakfast signifies rest, relaxation, and getting away from the busyness of life. We slow down and reconnect with those we love. Jesus wants us to also come to Him for our peace and quiet. The Lord even gave us His peace to help us overcome the trouble and fear we may face (John 14:27). We are also promised a complete Sabbath-type of rest as believers. A place of supernatural rest where we can cease from the weariness of human labor and effort and rely on God's ability to work through, in, and for us. We are encouraged to prioritize and protect the divine rest of God.

THE STONES

One of the most moving spiritual visions I have ever had involved stones. During my quiet time one morning, I was focusing on the concept of letting my worries go as Jesus tells us in His teachings. My eyes were closed as I was praying. Soon, I saw myself holding three small, smooth, gray stones in my right hand. My hand was in the pocket of the purple bathrobe I was wearing. Then, I took the stones out of my pocket and handed them to Jesus, who was facing me, also wearing a bathrobe. As I gave the Lord my stones, I saw that they had letters written on them. They were initials that represented the three main situations in my life that I had been concerned about.

The Lord took the gray stones from my hand as I gave them to Him. He then placed my stones in His own fluffy white robe pocket! Afterwards, I could hear His hand touching and holding the stones that were now in His pocket. I felt such relief knowing that those problems were now in His hands!

As the vision continued, Jesus and I were now at a local park, still in our bathrobes! But, lo and behold, those same three gray stones were back in my pocket again! I was frustrated with myself for carrying those stones of worry around again and not letting Jesus hold on to them for me. This time, instead of just handing the stones to the Lord, I threw them as far away from myself as I could!

They landed with plops in the large lake in the center of the park. Suddenly, Jesus walked into the lake, and carefully bent down to pick up the stones that I had just thrown. Just like before, He took them and placed them in the pocket of His fluffy, white robe. He was quiet, calm, and methodical in His movement. I was speechless and surprised at what had just occurred.

God is good. He won't criticize us if we happen to lose our peace and start to worry. God will faithfully lead us toward His vision through peace. We can find *shalom* in the truth that we are in the palm of the Father's hand (John 10:29). As we make decisions, we can lay them on the peace scale. In other words, if we have peace, we can take a step forward. If we do not have peace, perhaps it's not the best decision or the best time.

THE LOUNGE

I'd like to share one last vision. It's a bit silly and childish, but I think sometimes we tend to take God, church, and this whole religion thing a bit too seriously. Let's lighten up and laugh with the Lord occasionally. After all, we are encouraged to have childlike faith, not old fogey faith!

As I mentioned earlier, I grew up in the small country of Wales for a time. I used to spend many afternoons and weekends at my grandparents' white, two-story house. I remember singing, laughing, and playing outside or down in the cellar as a little girl, Welsh accent and all. In the evenings, my Nana and I would often lie on the couch in the living room. They called it the "lounge." To my delight, Nana would gently tickle or massage my feet as we watched detective shows or soap operas on the television together. I adored it!

I had my eyes closed and was listening to worship music one morning, and soon I saw myself in my Welsh grandparents' lounge, lying on the same sofa as I did with my Nana. The TV was on, and the smell of roast lamb wafted in from the kitchen. Grampa was napping in his armchair with the *Evening Post* newspaper covering his belly. I could hear Nana singing and banging some pots around as she prepared our dinner. I was lying in my usual spot on the couch, close to the window in the corner. Soon, I felt someone softly tickling my feet. I knew Nana was busy in the kitchen, so I lifted my head to see if my Mum had arrived home from work. To my surprise and delight, I saw the Lord Jesus Himself was tickling my feet! Before long, we switched spots on the couch, and Jesus let me tickle His feet! The worship song that I had been listening to ended, and so did the vision.

I shared all that to say that Jesus wants a personal relationship with all of us. If having my feet tickled brings me joy, then God is happy to do that. He delights in us as we delight in Him and is happy to give us the desires of our hearts that bring glory and goodness to Him.

As we rest in God, enjoy Him, and are childlike with Him, our anxiety will decrease as our peace increases. Which areas of your life could benefit from having more of God's peace? Can you visualize a way to connect and enjoy Jesus' company? Where would you go and what would you do if you could have a peaceful moment with Jesus? You can approach your good Father as a small child, in complete wonder, humility, playfulness, and trust.

LESSONS FROM THE LORD

There is so much to learn once we find our *supernatural* vision in such an *ordinary* world! The Holy Spirit can reveal wonderful truths even with our eyes closed. My spiritual visions, encounters, and dreams have improved my relationship with the Lord in ways I never could have imagined. These experiences have forever changed the way I view myself as well as God.

Through such visions and encounters, the Holy Spirit has demonstrated that our *purpose* is to become more like Jesus, be the light in a dark world, and live authentically as believers. As we pursue the path that God has designed for us, He will guide us to the precise *position* for our current preparation and future promotion. The Holy Spirit helps us cultivate a loving relationship with God and sense His *presence* within and around us. God loves us with *passion*, and we can allow the Lord to love others through us. The Holy Spirit moving in us can positively influence the earth and do damage to the kingdom of darkness as we live from our victorious *perspective* in heaven. We have been given supernatural *power.* We are equipped and able to fulfill our divine assignments, whether we realize it or not. All the wisdom, resources, and *provision* we need for life and ministry are being abundantly supplied. We can rest in God's goodness and enjoy His overwhelming *peace.*

Chapter 12

VARYING VIEWPOINTS

Jesus' ministry on the earth has given us a template of the lifestyle and vision that is now available to *every* believer. The Lord told us that what He did we could also do (John 14:12). Likewise, we are reminded that as Jesus is, so are we in the world (1 John 4:17).

Examining how Jesus followed the Father's vision gives us a greater understanding of how we can live our own lives with our spiritual eyes open. Again, the eight elements of spiritual vision are: *purpose, position, presence, passion, perspective, power, provision, and peace.* How exactly did Jesus walk in fullness and blessing in these areas?

JESUS' VIEWPOINT

Jesus' *purpose* was clear from the cradle to the cross. From His birth until His death, He walked in His purpose and calling. Due to His constant connection and communication with the Father, Jesus had clarity regarding His specific purpose. He was to find and help those in need and give them a rich and satisfying life (Luke 19:10; John 10:10). What would our day-to-day lives look like if we pursued our God-given appointments and assignments with such purpose?

Jesus had a dual *position* while He lived on the earth. He had an awareness of both the heavenly realm and the earthly realm. On one hand, He was silent, humble, and accepted punishment. He was born among men and lived among men. He was fully human. That is what we are referring to when we call Him the "Lamb" of God. However, He was also all-powerful and could have put an end to everyone who opposed Him in a second. He was also fully divine. That's what we mean when we call Him the "Lion of Judah." He knew what His position was on earth. He endured the shame, pain, and sin that humanity put on Him so He could divinely save them. What a beautiful picture of the posture we can have as His followers. As believers, we humble ourselves and allow God to elevate us. Yet we also have been given a position of power and authority over the earth, the enemy, and the conditions he may bring about. We exercise that position of power and authority with the Holy Spirit's leadership and love.

Jesus took special time away from the disciples and followers, alone in the *presence* of His Father, to pray. He even showed His friends a way they could pray, which is known as "The Lord's Prayer" or "Our Father." Jesus said He couldn't really do anything by Himself. Rather, He could only do what He saw the Father doing (John 5:19). This is a fascinating verse! The Son of God never acted independently of His Father. This means that He lived in constant communication (using His physical and spiritual senses) and presence with the Father. Imagine the breakthrough, influence, and impact that could happen through us if we would remain in daily interaction with the presence of our Father, God.

Passion is what fueled Jesus' thirty-three years on the earth. Passion is what pushed Him to endure death and hell for the lost. Passion energizes Him as He prays with us from heaven now. Passion (or love) is a powerful emotion that can make anyone do unbelievable things. As a mother will do anything to protect a child she loves, so can our passion for God and others motivate us to partner with God's vision and to further His Kingdom on the earth.

Jesus was able to keep the aspects of His earthly life in light of eternity. His schedule, commitments, relationships, and ministry were all motivated by the eternal ramifications in the spiritual realm. Due to His divine *perspective*, the Lord was effective and efficient in all that He did. Every moment of every day had a purpose and made an impact. Having a heavenly perspective will keep us on task and on track as we focus on the eternal and important rather than the temporal and urgent moments of our lives. While we don't ignore the realities of daily life or pretend our problems don't exist, we can face our mountains head-on, displaying the superior realities of God's Kingdom while still on earth.

Jesus told His disciples on the mountain at Galilee that all *power* and authority in heaven and earth was given to Him (Matthew 28:18). Jesus also gave that authority and power to His disciples to overcome the enemy (Luke 10:19). It was given as He sent out seventy-two of His followers to speak of the Kingdom, and to bring peace and healing to others. Power was supplied to them as they followed and fulfilled God's vision. That same power protects and propels us as we pursue God's ways and vision today (Ephesians 1:19-20).

As Jesus followed the Father's plan and vision, everything He needed was supplied! Doors were opened, people got involved, and *provision* came. A willing young mom, an understanding human dad, a forerunning cousin, and twelve eager learners participated. All the divine connections Jesus needed to fulfill His purpose came. A coin for taxes, a picnic lunch for thousands, an upper room for dinner, a donkey for a ride, perfume for burial, and an empty tomb to rise from were all furnished to fulfill the divine vision. The things that are needed to fulfill God's good plan will be faithfully provided to us.

Jesus walked in supernatural *peace*. The prophet Isaiah referred to Him as the "Prince of Peace" (Isaiah 9:6). He was seldom unsettled or worked up. As He implemented the Father's vision on earth, He was able to maintain a state of peace. Jesus taught that those who make peace with others are blessed (Matthew 5:9). Resting in divine peace will allow us to remain level-headed, calm, and blessed in the face of hardship, adversity, or chaos.

Christ was equipped and fully able to accomplish the Father's plan. He was fully aware of His purpose and position. He prioritized presence with the Father. He lived and died passionately on the earth. He cultivated a heavenly perspective as He walked in power and authority. His every need for life and ministry was divinely provided. He maintained and brought a mindset of peace to the world. I dare say that we, too, are equipped and fully able to accomplish the Father's destiny for our lives.

We *can* chase those fierce giants and move those massive mountains even with our eyes shut if we continue to keep our *spiritual* eyes wide open!

BELIEVING IS SEEING

At this point, you might be thinking, "That's fine for you, Julia. I'm just not into all this envisioning and imagination stuff." I completely understand that. Many people have a relationship with God that is more dominant in knowledge and wisdom than in spirit or feeling. All of the ways we relate to God are valid and vital. Yet as Christians, we all have a secret longing and vision for more. We realize that there are things available to us that go beyond our present experience. Our present experience with God and His Word isn't the climax of how far we can go in our relationship or expectations with Him.

Our pursuit as children of God is to continue searching for the unknown, discovering the hidden, and finding the unseen as we remain hungry for more revelation of the Holy Spirit. I would challenge you to open your mind to the idea of broadening your spiritual senses to see and hear more from God. Even if you don't have a specific vision for your future at this moment, you can act using spiritual foresight in faith. Walking by faith means trusting God's promises and plans even when we *can't* see them with our eyes.

In the world, most is believed only when it is seen. But in the Kingdom of God, many things can appear upside-down. Jesus told us the last shall be first, the weak will be strong, the sad will receive joy, and the lonely will become families. We are promised that those who have not seen but believe anyway will be blessed (John 20:29). Jesus explains that if we *believe* first, we will *then* see the glory of God (John 11:40). What exactly is the glory of God? It's the manifested excellence, power, majesty, and presence of God. Wow! Who wouldn't want to see that?

The secret to seeing such goodness and faithfulness of God on display in our lives is to adopt a visionary lifestyle that can perceive a victory *before* it happens; a mindset that can visualize already receiving what was prayed for; the spiritual foresight to envision *already* having the promises of God. This way of living frees us from the limits of just our physical eyesight.

Faith is the first requirement before we are able to see anything. Hebrews 11:1 gives us an explanation of faith:

> *"Faith shows the reality of what we hope for; it is the evidence of things we cannot see."* (Hebrews 11:1 NLT)

Faith is not based on human sight but on our spiritual *insight* of knowing who God is, as well as the *foresight* to see into the future. This is why Paul reminded the Church to live by faith and not by sight (2 Corinthians 5:7).

Faith requires us to look beyond what we see with our physical eyes because faith is visionary. Moses, Abraham, David, and Paul were all visionaries. They had the ability to envision all that God promised long before it happened. They were able to look forward in faith because they knew God would deliver on His promises.

Abraham expected more, so he looked for it (Hebrews 11:10). More was possible than what he saw with his physical eyes.

How can we increase our faith to behold a future we have yet to see? The New Testament tells us that faith comes by hearing the Word. As we increase our intake of God's Word, described as a seed, it will grow in our spirits and produce a "harvest." Even if we're not seeking divine dreams, encounters, or visions, we can all increase our faith levels and keep our spiritual eyes open to see God's greater vision unfold. **In the world, *seeing* is believing, but in God's Kingdom, *believing* is seeing.**

OBSCURED VIEWPOINTS

Since there is a definite correlation between our natural sight and our spiritual sight, let's examine some of the physical ways our ability to see can become obscured, and apply that to our spiritual sight. Some of the more common optical conditions that limit our vision include: *nearsightedness, farsightedness, astigmatism, cataracts,* and *color blindness*. Let's discuss a few of these without getting too technical; Lord knows I'm not a doctor!

Nearsightedness is as the name describes. It's when an individual can see objects clearly when they are near or close to them, but objects that are at a distance appear blurred. For example, you might be able to read a book without any problems, but watching TV from across the room will look blurry.

Farsightedness is just the opposite. An individual can see objects clearly that are at a distance, but up close, they appear blurred.

These individuals can read road signs clearly when driving but might find reading a phone difficult.

Astigmatism is when the surface of the lens or cornea is not spherical, but egg-shaped. The eye then focuses on two separate points instead of one. This causes blurred vision at near and far distances and difficulty seeing at night.

Cataracts cause the clouding of the lens in one eye or both. This causes a person's vision to become cloudy, blurry, or dim. Colors can look faded, or lights can appear too bright. Halos can even appear around lights.

Color blindness prevents individuals from seeing colors the way most others do. It makes distinguishing distinct colors and shades difficult. Some people can't tell the difference between red and green, while others can't differentiate between blue and yellow. Most people who are color-blind don't realize they are, as people tend to get used to the way they see color.

Now that we know what these physical eye conditions are, let's see how these conditions could also affect our spiritual sight. Being nearsighted in the spiritual sense could describe a person who only has short-term vision. They don't have the patience or foresight to see the future with their eyes of faith. They are governed by the here and now, and by what is most prominently displayed in their life. We can all suffer from spiritual nearsightedness for a season. If we stay nearsighted permanently, though, our eyes of faith stay underdeveloped.

Being farsighted, in the spiritual sense, could characterize a person who only lives for tomorrow and cannot enjoy today. This kind of person has what could be called "destination disease." They believe they will be happy only when a certain milestone or point in time is reached. They will be happy when they get married, when they have kids, when they can retire, when they move, and so on. The problem with this condition is that they cannot enjoy the process or journey of learning and growing along the way. They spend their whole lives pursuing what they don't yet have instead of valuing and enjoying what they do have now. To be honest, I used to fall into this category. I used to fantasize about living by the beach, getting a fancier home, having grandchildren, being debt free, and others. There was nothing wrong with wanting those things, but they were preventing me from thanking God for the blessings of here and now. I have learned how to approach each day in anticipation of what I will learn and how God can use me.

Spiritual astigmatism could be compared to double-mindedness or double devotion. It could describe someone who has one foot in church and the other in willful sin. This causes divided attention and devotion between the ways of the world and the ways of God's Kingdom. Again, these are conditions that can befall us all temporarily with the ups and downs of life, but if they become permanent, they can really skew our vision.

Spiritual cataracts can cloud God's Word, voice, and vision. The person of Jesus and the voice of the Holy Spirit becomes dimmer and lower. Things this person used to enjoy and understand about God don't interest them anymore. The brightness of loving God has diminished, and halos of light appear around things they once thought were too dark. This is a scary place to remain in permanently and requires a spiritual awakening to overcome.

Spiritual color blindness is deceptive because the individual doesn't realize they have a false perception of what they see. How they view God's Word, will, and ways can be jaded. They find it difficult to differentiate between what God is saying and what the enemy is speaking and showing them. They have a challenging time knowing what is from God and what is not.

If Jesus was able to heal a person's physical sight, surely He can heal our spiritual sight if we ask. The Holy Spirit is more than willing to guide us as we desire to change our perspective and correct our spiritual eyes of misunderstanding. We would be wise to examine the state of our spiritual sight with the same effort we take care of and correct our physical sight.

Chapter 13

TWELVE KEYS THAT UNLOCK SPIRITUAL VISION

The One who created us wants to communicate with us daily! Visions are just *one* of the many ways that God speaks to His people. God can speak through His Word, our thoughts, other believers, or even by feelings of peace. God doesn't give us dreams and visions just to frustrate us. As He gives us visions to pursue, the Holy Spirit will give us the energy, strength, and power to fulfill them. God has envisioned remarkable things for you. Ask Him to reveal them to you however He chooses.

Perhaps that's a prompting or a stirring deep inside of you. Maybe that's hearing clearly from God as you read and study Scripture. It may be that you close your eyes and see divinely inspired pictures. There's no perfect or right way to hear from God or experience the presence of Jesus. What matters is that you are seeking more of God.

As I reflected on how my spiritual eyesight unblurred over time, I identified several keys that opened my eyes of faith. I am excited to share these with you and I pray you give these ideas and activities an open-minded try with the hope and expectation that you will begin to clarify your Kingdom vision!

When it comes to having sharp vision physically, or when we refer to 20/20 vision, that does not mean an individual has perfect vision. It means a person can see an object's normal sharpness and clarity about twenty feet away. As you study these twelve keys, remember to strive for progress, not perfection. We may never see with complete clarity this side of heaven. Our eyes have yet to see all the wonderful things God is preparing for us, but there are many things that God will reveal to us by His Spirit, so let's keep pressing on in faith to observe all that we can.

KEY #1 – PLANT THE SEED OF SCRIPTURE

God's process for growth and development are the three phases of gardening: seed, time, and harvest (Genesis 8:22). In other words, everything in God's Kingdom (or garden) starts out in seed form before it matures into a plant or a tree. After several weeks or seasons, the plant or tree eventually produces fruit.

The Bible says that the **Word** itself is a seed. Jesus tells the Parable of the Sower in Matthew 13, Mark 4, and Luke 8. Here is how Jesus describes it in Matthew:

> *"Then he told them many things in parables, saying: 'A farmer went out to sow his seed. As he was scattering the seed, some fell along the path, and the birds came and ate it up. Some fell on rocky places, where it did not have much soil. It sprang up quickly, because the soil was shallow. But when the sun came up, the plants were scorched, and they withered because they had no*

root. Other seed fell among thorns, which grew up and choked the plants. Still other seed fell on good soil, where it produced a crop—a hundred, sixty or thirty times what was sown'" (Matthew 13:3-8 NIV).

Some people don't believe or understand the Bible at all, as the birds (representing the enemy) steal it from along the path. Others receive Scripture with joy for a while but don't develop any roots, so they dry up and wither when problems come. Some receive the Word of God, but the message is crowded out by thorns of distractions and weeds of worry, preventing them from producing any real or lasting fruit. However, people who honor, understand, and accept the good news (nurturing the seed in the good soil) eventually produce a great harvest!

Before we can produce any kind of harvest in our spiritual lives, we need to honor, understand, and accept the Word of God as our seed. Once that seed has been planted in our spirits, it needs time, care, and nourishment to grow a healthy, deep root system. Finally, after seasons of preparation and development, the fruit of the Spirit will be apparent in our lives (Galatians 5:2-23).

Maybe you feel uncertain of the future because you can't recall any significant vision God has given you to pursue. In reality, you have already received a divine vision from God. It is seen in the Bible. So, we look there first. Meditating on Scripture is one of the first and foremost ways that God wants to communicate His vision with you. The author of Psalm 119 prayed for his eyes to be opened so he could see wonderful things from God's Law or instruction and to look away from worthless things (Psalm 119:18, 37). Interpreting the Bible accurately is essential to finding God's vision and living a victorious Christian life.

Activation Activity:

1. Study the three accounts of the Parable of the Sower in the Gospels: Matthew 13:1-23; Mark 4:1-34; and Luke 8:4-18.

2. Reflect and pray about the following: In which phase of farming the seed of God's Word into your heart do you see yourself? Are there any parts of the Bible that you are struggling to believe for yourself? How have difficult circumstances and situations kept you from staying in God's Word? What is distracting you from spending time reading the Bible? How could you set aside some time soon to plant more of God's Word into your heart?

3. Look for any signs, clues, or parts that stand out to you as you read and study the Bible. These may be areas that the Holy Spirit is highlighting to you. Dig in deeper to those verses and stories to discover what God may be pointing out to you.

4. As you are looking *in* the Word of God, remember to look *up* to perceive what the Holy Spirit is revealing to you. Look *in* your own heart (your garden) to inspect your fruit. Look *behind* to reflect on all the ways that God has been faithful to provide in the past. Finally, look *forward* to the things you believe but don't see with your physical eyes yet.

KEY #2 – LEARN TO WAIT WELL

The Hebrew verb "to wait," used in the Old Testament, conveys a more complex meaning than when we think of waiting in the English language. The biblical interpretation of waiting is looking eagerly for something, hoping, longing for, or *expecting*. When the scriptures speak of waiting on the Lord, that act of waiting is not a passive activity but an active looking, longing for, and expectation of the Lord! Expect provision, expect blessing, expect God to show up, and expect your spiritual eyes to be completely open.

Biblical waiting expects and acts *before* the intended result appears.

The prophet Samuel hosted a party, prepared a meal, and set aside a plate for the new king's anticipated arrival (1 Samuel 10:22-24). A childless woman was told to get the nursery ready in anticipation of becoming pregnant (Isaiah 54:2). The disciples gathered in the upper room and waited indefinitely for the coming Holy Spirit (Acts 1:13-14). Are we willing to wait indefinitely and expectantly for God?

The British evangelist Smith Wigglesworth often said, "Faith is an act." When we wait for God in eager anticipation and expectation, we are moving by faith. We are actively expecting Him to respond. It can be difficult to wait on God and make peace with His pace. Remember that waiting time is not wasted time but our preparation time. In our waiting, God is working.

Activation Activity:

    1. Try to keep your spiritual antennae up. This means noticing

and perceiving what God may be trying to show you. Look for the ways the Holy Spirit may be leading you in certain circumstances or conversations and begin to respond. Which people may God be highlighting to you throughout the day? This could be a simple "Thank you God for showing me that," or "I think You may be trying to show me this, God, but I'm not sure."

2. Read Isaiah 43:19. Ask God what new things He wants to do in your life. Try to imagine and envision those things. How can you participate while waiting for God to do those new things? Get creative and really see what that would involve and entail on your part and on God's part.

3. As you get up in the morning to start your day, tell God what you are hoping and waiting for that day. If we believe God is going to show us things, then our eyes will be more likely to notice and perceive the little (and big) things God wants to show us.

KEY #3 – BECOME FULL OF FAITH

Faith is not blind—it's visionary! If we use our eyes of faith, we will be able to take steps of obedience toward the vision God has for us, even if we are a bit afraid. Our spiritual sight gives us eyes to see what may not make sense to our physical eyes. Just as Abraham took one step at a time toward the land that God would show him, so can we broaden our sight to see ahead with our eyes of faith.

I've heard it said that people don't go to hell because of *sin;* they go because of *unbelief.* As believers, it's our privilege and responsibility to take God at His Word and believe what He says is true. In the context of seeing with our spiritual eyes, we can actually *believe* that God wants to reveal Himself to us. We can *believe* that we will see Him moving in our lives today. King David exclaimed,

> *"[What, what would have become of me] had I **not believed that I would see** the Lord's goodness in the land of the living?"* (Psalm 27:13 AMPC, emphasis added)

Jesus told the two blind men in Matthew that because of their *faith,* their miracle would happen (Matthew 9:29). What we ask for in prayer is granted to us when we believe (Mark 11:24).

Although her brother Lazarus was lying dead in the tomb, Martha still believed in God's truth, saying "even now" I know Jesus can perform this miracle. She tried to get Jesus there in time, hoping for a healing, but because of her "even now" faith, she witnessed a resurrection!

God reveals His vision to us over time. We may only see part of the vision at first. As we respond in faith to what God is showing us, the vision becomes clearer. Discerning God's vision requires patience as we reflect and process what we are perceiving. Our faith will then allow us to embrace what we find.

Activation Activity:

    1. Faith is grown by *hearing* (not just reading) the Word of

God (Romans 10:17). Try reading the Bible aloud (instead of silently). Alternatively, listen to the Bible being read either through an app, video, or a friend.

2. Meditate on verses by reading aloud until you can almost recite them. Several scriptures are included at the end of this book to help with this.

3. Pray (aloud) about those verses with God.

KEY #4 – SAY IT AGAIN

The Bible is full of wisdom regarding the words we speak. I have heard it said that our lives are the sum of our words, good or bad. As Christians, we can use our words to encourage, build up, and heal (and certainly not the opposite). We can also speak in alignment with God's Word as well as with His vision. Our words really do carry creative power. Proverbs 18 reminds us that...

> *"Death and life are in the power of the **tongue**, and those who love it and indulge it will eat its fruit and bear **the consequences of their words.**"* (Proverbs 18:21 AMP, emphasis added)

Paul told the churches that if they believed, they should also speak (2 Corinthians 4:13). This is because believing and speaking are intertwined in the lifestyle of believers. It can be said that saying produces seeing. Let's look at two examples of speaking an intended result *before* the outcome. First, the young shepherd David, before defeating the giant Goliath, *spoke* in faith, saying,

> *"You come against me with sword and spear and javelin,*
> *but I come against you in the name of the Lord Almighty,*
> *the God of the armies of Israel, whom you have defied.*
> *This day the Lord will deliver you into my hands, ..."* (1 Samuel 17:45-46 NIV)

David spoke of his triumph before it occurred, which may have seemed arrogant, immature, or foolish to bystanders. However, David truly had faith and belief in how his words aligned with God's vision for his people and God gave him the strength to defeat Goliath.

In the Gospel of Mark, a woman who had been bleeding for twelve years heard about Jesus. When she found Him, she said,

> *"If I just touch His clothing, I will get well"* (Mark 5:28 AMP).

On this occasion, the woman *spoke* what she hoped would happen before it did. She looked with her eyes of faith to see what was possible once she made contact with Jesus. Both are prime examples of speaking by faith before seeing.

We can also learn how God speaks to us by learning His special language. Again, one of the primary ways God communicates with us is through His written Word. However, God can choose to speak to us through other means. For some that can be images or pictures. For others, it can be an inner voice or prompting of the Holy Spirit. God can even speak to us through our circumstances and through other people.

As we begin to become more aware of the unusual ways God can speak, we will be more apt to notice when He communicates. Have you ever bought a new car and then suddenly noticed that multiple people have the same car you just bought? It's not because you and everyone else ran out and bought the same car on the same day. Rather, now you are more aware of that car and more apt to recognize it. It's the same with God. As you learn to recognize some of the ways the Holy Spirit wants to speak to you, you will become more aware of them.

Activation Activity:

To begin believing before you see, and to activate the powerful spiritual principle of speaking by faith, below are two sets of declarations. These biblically based declarations can activate your faith to awaken your spiritual eyesight. I recommend you say them aloud daily or weekly. Refer to the appendix for supplementary declarations.

10 General Visionary Verses

1. In the Kingdom, believing is seeing.

2. I believe I shall see the Lord's goodness in my life.

3. I am increasing in spiritual wisdom, eyesight, and insight.

4. God has poured out His Spirit, so I can speak, see, and dream!

5. I have a clear vision from the Lord, and He gives me grace to see it come to pass.

6. I notice, recognize, and reflect on what I see.

7. God will always provide for the vision He gives me.

8. Everything has already been provided; I just haven't seen it yet.

9. I share God's vision with others to encourage them.

10. My vision for the future gives me power for the present.

10 Specific Visionary Scriptures

1. I encounter God by **faith** (Hebrews 11:6).

2. I use my **imagination** to activate my faith (2 Corinthians 4:18).

3. God will do more than I can even ask or **imagine** (Ephesians 3:20).

4. The Holy Spirit works powerfully and miraculously in me as I **believe** (Galatians 3:5).

5. I am being inwardly transformed by the Holy Spirit through a total reformation of how I think. I am renewing my **mind** according to the will and Word of God (Romans 12:2).

6. The eyes of my heart and of my **imagination** are enlightened to **see** the hope, purpose, inheritance, and power that I have been called into (Ephesians 1:18).

7. I have the **mind** of Christ and the wisdom and knowledge of God. I am guided by His thoughts, purposes, and understanding. I am learning how to yield to His way of thinking (1 Corinthians 2:16).

8. I have **insight,** wisdom, ideas, divine strategies, and solutions (James 1:5-8).

9. The Spirit of **Truth** has come, and He is guiding me into all **truth** (John 16:13).

10. God is doing new things! I will recognize, **see**, and partner with God in them (Isaiah 43:19).

KEY #5 – PRAY THROUGH

Each individual is designed with unique love languages and communication styles, which means we all become close friends with God through different avenues. However, when we get up close and personal with our Father, with Jesus, and with the Holy Spirit, it always involves a mix of prayer, community, and quality time.

As we approach our heavenly Father in prayer for increased spiritual vision, or for anything else, we consider that God is present and wants to listen to us. There's no need to apologize, rush, explain ourselves, or feel embarrassed. Our Father loves and enjoys us as

His children, appreciative of our time and attention. We can trust that He will reward us as we seek Him.

When we spend time in prayer, we don't need to *beg* God but to ask in *confident trust* that we will receive answers (Hebrews 4:16; 11:6). Believe that prayer is productive, worthwhile, and influential. Trust that God hears, and that He is working on our behalves. After praying, we will receive the right answer at the appropriate time, so we thank God for working as we eagerly anticipate how He will respond to our questions, worries, or desires (Mark 11:24). Paul stressed the importance of cultivating an attitude of thankfulness. He taught the church at Colossae to overflow with gratitude and to be thankful during times of prayer (Colossians 2:17; 3:15; 4:2).

As we close our eyes in prayer, we shut our eyes to the here and now. We tune in to God's realm to see what He wants to show us.

There is a beautiful verse in the book of Jeremiah where God promises that as we pray to Him, He will answer us by *showing* us great and hidden things (Jeremiah 33:3). Let's remember to approach God with faith and expectancy, but also with *thankfulness* for all that He has done and continues to do.

Activation Activity:

1. Write out a prayer to your heavenly Father asking for what you are seeking in this season of your life. Perhaps you'd like more clarity regarding a decision you need to make. Maybe you want to have a better idea or perspective of God's purpose and vision for your life. Maybe you are seeking advice regarding a particular relationship. Perhaps

you are suffering from one of the common spiritual eyesight conditions we mentioned in chapter twelve. As you prepare your prayer, remember to:

- Ask the Father in confidence with faith.

- Believe that your prayer will be heard and is productive and powerful.

- Approach God with an attitude of gratitude.

- Read your prayer aloud to the Father, asking in Jesus' name.

KEY #6 – GET YOUR WORSHIP ON

Worship is one of the most fruitful ways to begin seeing with the eyes of our spirits.

I love the Christian author A.W. Tozer's description of worship. He writes, "Worship...is to feel in the heart and express in an appropriate manner a humbling but delightful sense of admiring awe."[1]

The Hebrew meaning of the word "worship" is to bow down in reverence. The first mention of the word "worship" in the Bible can be found in Genesis 22.

> *"And Abraham said to his servants, 'Settle down and stay here with the donkey; the young man and I will go yonder and **worship** [God], and we will come back to you'"* (Genesis 22:5 AMP, emphasis added).

In this chapter, the Lord tested Abraham by seeing if he would obey Him by sacrificing his promised son. Abraham responded by going up to the mountain with his son, Isaac, but telling his servants that they would *both* return after they had worshipped God. Furthermore, Abraham told his son that God would supply the animal for the sacrifice. When the time came for the sacrifice, Abraham lifted his knife to kill his son, but the angel of the Lord appeared to Abraham announcing that God knew Abraham feared and revered God since he did not hold anything back from Him, not even his son. God went on to bless and multiply Abraham.

We were created to worship God, our Creator, even though it may be difficult to worship during times of hurt and sacrifice. Jesus tells us that He is looking for those who will worship genuinely in Spirit and in truth (John 4:23). Maybe you're not used to worshipping or praising God at all. Perhaps your worship time has become routine or mundane. You may find yourself easily distracted while praising the Lord. Authentic worship is not always convenient or easy, but that's why it's called a "sacrifice" of praise. We give our attention and affection to the One who gave it all for us.

Scripture tells us that the Lord *inhabits* the praises of His people, so it is a biblical promise that when we praise God, He appears! The Hebrew word *yasah,* which is translated as "inhabit" in Psalm 22:3, means to dwell, remain, sit, or abide. When we focus on the Lord in worship, praise, and adoration, He is sitting and abiding with us.

Whether worshipping God has been a natural and habitual part of your relationship with God, or it's something new and uncomfortable, keep at it. As you worship, you are training your spiritual eyes to focus on the presence and goodness of the Lord. This will allow your spirit to be more attentive to the promptings of the Holy Spirit.

Activation Activity:

1. Find a quiet place to be alone with God for at least fifteen minutes. This may be the first thing in the morning or right before bed. Choose whatever is a suitable time for you.

2. Play some worship music that praises God and inspires you.

3. Start singing along (if the music has words) and praising the Lord for all that He has done for you.

4. If you haven't already, close your eyes.

5. Picture yourself standing in front of Jesus, singing directly to Him.

6. If you start to picture Jesus in your mind, focus on what else you can see or hear with Jesus. Can you see Him doing or saying anything? Don't try to force something, just let the Spirit lead you.

- If you get distracted or frustrated, simply open your eyes, focus back on the song, and continue to thank and praise God. For we enter His courts with thanksgiving and praise (Psalm 100:4).

- It might take a few songs before you perceive anything, as it can take a bit of time to move from your natural reasoning to a spiritual focus.

- If nothing happens this time, keep practicing. Try different songs or styles.

- Once you have tried this a few times privately, try it the next time you're in a group setting, like at a Sunday morning church service or with a small group.

I do not recommend trying this activity while you are driving for obvious reasons!

KEY #7 – JOT IT DOWN

I used to hear people talk about how great journaling was, but I never felt inclined to do it myself. I guess it was because it reminded me of being a teenager and writing about my silly ordeals in a diary, so I resisted the idea for quite a while. However, one day I decided, by faith, to try it. I had been reading a book about how to hear from God, and the author recommended asking God what was on His heart and then writing down what you felt He was saying to you. Wow! After the download of words, images, and messages from God that day, I have enjoyed journaling ever since!

Remembering and recording what God has done for us is something the Israelites practiced very well. Whether it was building an altar, placing some stones, or naming a certain place, it was especially important for them to remember the miracles and mercies of God. In the Bible, we read that the prophet Samuel cried to the Lord for Israel and that the Lord answered him by defeating the Philistines. Samuel was so grateful to God for intervening that he took a stone and called it "Ebenezer," which means "stone of help" (1 Samuel 7:9-12). This would serve as a visual reminder that God heard and responded to prayer. In the same manner, when we write down any answered prayers, messages, or insight that we receive by spending time with the Father, we are acknowledging that God hears us and speaks to us.

Journaling is a way to record what we have received, and sets us up for future revelation.

Journaling is also a way to process what the Lord is showing us. As we write down (or even draw) any messages, images, visions, dreams, or insights we receive, we can ask God questions and grow in our faith. Sometimes things we envision and journal about are for a future time. We write them down and they are fulfilled later. We have seen many of the prophets' writings come to pass within the Bible, yet several of the Old Testament prophets' writings have still not happened, but we trust they will. What joy and endurance are revealed when we wait in faith for the promises and insights we are given! Journaling is a beautiful reminder of where we have been, where we are, and where we can be one day.

Once we have written down ideas that we think are from the Holy Spirit, we can then revisit those notes and determine if what we heard really was from the Lord. When we record how God has answered our prayers, walked with us, and taught us, we can see how faithful He is. I don't know about you, but I have trouble remembering things at times. I certainly do *not* want to forget all that the Lord has shared with me or done for me.

Activation Activity:

If you don't have a journal yet, then go buy one! Any small notebook will do. It doesn't have to be fancy. I personally use those old-school composition notebooks with the black-and-white covers. Then, during your next prayer and worship time, try the following:

1. Find a safe, focused place and settle your mind. Whether that means quiet or gentle music, or with background sounds that soothe you, make sure you are free of distractions. Turn off notifications on your phone.

2. Close your physical eyes, and look with your spiritual eyes, believing to see.

3. Listen with your spiritual ears to hear what the Lord might be saying.

4. Continue to focus on any images you see in your mind or things you hear speaking to your heart. Keep looking and listening as long as you can.

5. Jot down any images, pictures, thoughts, words, or impressions you have heard or seen in your journal.

6. Ask God questions about what you saw, heard, or felt. For example, what do these images mean? How do they apply to me? What are You trying to tell me here? Can You affirm this with any scriptures? Write down what you feel are His answers.

7. Do some research into what you saw or heard. For example, search for Bible verses that include key words or topics

from what you envisioned or heard. Maybe research images you saw or messages you heard for consistent symbolism or meaning. Then add any pertinent information to your journal.

8. Try this several times until you get used to the process.

9. Go back and occasionally re-read what you wrote previously.

KEY #8 – MANAGE AND MULTIPLY

There is a story that Jesus tells in the book of Matthew often referred to as the Parable of the Talents. It describes how three servants handled money their master gave them. Two traded or invested some money and gained more. The third servant feared losing the money, so he hid it—which means he didn't gain any interest either (Matthew 25:14-30). The master himself calls the first two servants faithful and trustworthy while referring to the third servant as wicked, lazy, and idle. The parable ends with this stern warning:

"To those who use well what they are given, even more will be given, and they will have an abundance. But from those who do nothing, even what little they have will be taken away." (Matthew 25:29 NLT)

At first glance, this might seem unreasonable and cruel, but the master in the story is rewarding excellence over mediocrity. Likewise, Jesus rewards our ability to manage and even multiply what we've been given. We are supposed to *steward* our resources, gifts, abilities, talents, and callings to the greatest extent possible for God's honor and glory. A steward is morally responsible for the use of money, time, , or other resources. So, a steward is one who responsibly manages such things.

Considering this parable, another key to clarify your spiritual vision is to steward (or manage) what you have already envisioned or seen in the past. In the physical realm, muscles increase in size as we use them. In the spiritual realm, there is also the capacity for increase through use. Yet it's not so we can build our own kingdom, but so others can benefit from God's Kingdom. The more we remember, reflect, appreciate, and use what we have been given, the more we will be given, and we will be able to give to others.

As we use and steward what the Lord has already shared, shown, or revealed to us, we will be given increase.

Our recorded journal entries can serve as our Ebenezer stone like Samuel's. This stone was a symbol and dedicated monument of God's goodness. Faith pleases God, and this type of stewarding is an aspect of believing. In Zechariah 4:10, the messenger of God told the people *not* to despise the day of small beginnings because the Lord was happy to see the work begin. Small things are gifts from God and indicators of greater things to come. Recognizing, appreciating, and honoring insignificant things in the beginning phases pleases the Lord. Sometimes we pray for a tree, but God will give us an acorn. Oftentimes His answers come in seed form. That's why we must be faithful to cultivate, tend, and manage the fertile soil of our hearts and spirits so the seeds of our visions can grow.

Activation Activity:

1. Sometimes to discern our future, we need to look at our past. As a means of stewarding what you have already received, write down (in your journal) any goals, dreams, and desires that you have envisioned for yourself or your family in the past. Include any encouraging words that others have spoken to you. What did you enjoy doing when you were young? What do you think God created you to do or be?

2. Try to recall any significant answered prayers. Begin a log and record the dates they were answered if you can remember. If not, you can estimate. The important thing is that you are remembering and recalling God's faithfulness.

3. Pray about what God wants you to do next. Which step of faith does God want you to take toward a particular vision or goal? How might God be preparing you for the next phase or season that is coming? What did God say a while back that you may have ignored or forgotten? Write down any impressions, ideas, or feelings you get.

4. Talk to God about what you have written down (dreams, desires, goals, etc.) and ask for even more insight from the Holy Spirit. Sometimes we want God to speak to us when we haven't really listened to what He said the last time!

5. Read aloud what you have written down as a way of speaking and believing in the spiritual realm before seeing anything manifest in the physical realm.

KEY #9 – CHOOSE THE CORRECT FILTER

What are you really focusing on every day? How can you stop and take time to see the supernatural signs and traces of God in your ordinary world? How can you see the mountains of disappointment and discouragement removed? By looking through the correct filter, you will see God's provision and hand in your life. Search for evidence of Him working in the mundane and the normal. How are you envisioning yourself? Do you see yourself as a *victim* or a *victor?* Do you picture yourself alone or as God's precious child? How do you view your family and community? Are things *hopeless* or *hopeful?*

Just as we may use filters to improve photographs we've taken, let's try applying a filter of divine expectancy, possibility, and grace to other people, situations, and even ourselves.

Seeing others through God's lens helps us find the "gold" in them. We can see people for what they will become, not what their past says they are. Jesus saw what His disciples could become, not what they were currently. Begin to see the people you prayed for as changed. Begin to see today's sacrifices in view of tomorrow's rewards.

The twelve spies that were sent out to explore Canaan interpreted their situation through a different filter than Joshua and Caleb. The spies looked at the circumstances through their inadequacy, believing they were not strong enough to conquer the powerful Canaanites. However, Caleb chose to look at the situation through the filter of God's power and might. Learning to look at our lives through a filter that aligns with the truth and the message of Jesus gives us a heavenly perspective.

Do you ever imagine how God can use your gifts to make a difference in the Kingdom? What do you see yourself doing or creating with God?

Activation Activity:

1. Take some time to reflect on and journal about the following: How do I see myself? How do I regard my family? How do I consider my community? How do I view my role at church? How do I regard others? How do I perceive God? Where do I see God working in my life?

2. Do you notice any patterns or themes in your answers? Ask the Holy Spirit to reveal any false or misleading filters you may be looking through. Ask Him to help you filter what you see through His truth and love. Try applying a spiritual filter of possibility and grace to your answers to the above questions.

KEY #10 – TAKE A TEST

Now it's time to brainstorm as we answer some vital questions to help us sharpen our supernatural vision as well as focus on what God's vision may be for our lives. Think beyond God's general vision and will for all humanity (that we have a personal relationship with His Son, that we walk in love, and that we bring the message of truth into every place and situation we find ourselves). We are referring to more *specific* Kingdom visions and divine assignments that have been uniquely planned by God for us.

Activation Activity:

Our "super" sight can transform and define our lives by giving us revelation in the areas of purpose, position, presence, passion, perspective, power, provision, and peace. Get a pen and paper out and brainstorm about the following:

1. What are some things that give me a sense of **purpose** or accomplishment?

2. In which direction would I like to see my life go and where is God **positioning** me?

3. When do I feel the closest to God or sense His **presence** the most?

4. Which types of activities energize and motivate me or fill me with **passion**?

5. When am I most focused on maintaining an eternal and heavenly **perspective**?

6. When have I really felt God's supernatural **power** working in me?

7. Where have I seen God's **provision** in my life when I needed it most?

8. What causes me to feel most grounded and at **peace**?

Once you have gotten some fresh ideas from the Holy Spirit, you can use the "Kingdom Vision Checklist" at the back of this book to help you determine if a certain idea, activity, or endeavor includes most of the above qualities.

KEY #11 – CREATE A VISION BOARD

If we can envision our future first in our spirits, it will more likely manifest in the physical realm.

We've mentioned before that as believers, many times we must believe before we see. Jesus taught that we are blessed when we don't see but can still believe (John 20:29). Nevertheless, pictures have power because they focus us. A vision board can serve as a useful tool to help us see physically what we are believing in spiritually. Scott and I created our first vision board a few years ago. It was inspiring and therapeutic. We have kept it hanging up since we made it. Seeing some of the things we added to our vision board come to fruition has solidified the truth that seeing with our eyes of faith precedes seeing something in the natural.

Activation Activity:

1. Reflect on your insights from several of the previous activation activities.

2. Pray about the things that God is unveiling and revealing to you regarding your spiritual eyesight. What are you seeing now? What do you want to see?

3. Gather several images, ideas, concepts, examples, words,

and phrases that represent those visions for yourself (and perhaps your family). These images can be on paper or computer depending upon your preference and availability.

4. Decide whether to create a virtual board or a traditional board and go for it! Pinterest is wonderful for making a virtual board or visit your local craft store for poster board, stickers, and other needed supplies. The internet is full of ideas and examples of vision boards. Once ready, add all your items to the board.

5. Place your board where you can glance at it often and be inspired.

KEY #12 – WRITE A VISION STATEMENT

Now that you've had the chance to study, pray, reflect, worship, and journal to refine your Kingdom vision, let's refine your focus even more. It's time to write your vision statement! If that sounds daunting, I understand. As you listen to the voice of the Holy Spirit and respond with faith, your vision will become clearer. It's even likely your statement may be revised over time as you gain more clarity. Just begin to envision your life with God. Visualize what your life will look like once the mountains of stress, depression, lack, and disappointment are removed. Trust that God will reveal more of the vision as you take steps of obedience in faith.

A vision statement is a sentence or two that describes your aspirations for your future. It may include your purpose, goals, values, growth, outcomes, and impact. It serves as a way to envision your future with God. Having a clear, meaningful vision statement can help motivate you. It can prompt action and release your imagination. For inspiration and examples, you might want to look at the vision statements of businesses or organizations that touch or impress you.

Your vision statement should include:

- **The actions you will take.**

- **The people, places, or things you will impact.**

- **How or why you will accomplish this.**

For example, a tea and coffee company might have the following vision statement:

> *"Collaborate to roast great-tasting, organic coffee and tea products with companies that support the well-being of all people."*

A vision statement for this book could be:

> *"Encourage and equip believers in developing their spiritual vision to fuel their future."*

Activation Activity:

1. Make a list of your short and long-term goals.

2. Make a list of your priorities, purposes, talents, and passions.

3. Which outcomes, results or impact do you want to achieve?

4. How will God change and develop you through this?

5. What might God want to create or accomplish through you?

6. Who might God want to help through you?

7. How will God help you do this?

8. Describe God's perfect future for yourself and your family.

9. Write out what you think God's vision for your life is right now.

10. Construct your vision statement using the answers to the above questions (and others) and by asking for the Holy Spirit's wisdom and guidance. Revise and rewrite as needed.

The above twelve keys will help unlock your spiritual eyesight. By spending time in God's Word, as well as in prayer and worship, we can get a clearer picture of God's vision for our future. Journaling and remembering what God has done builds our faith for a brighter tomorrow. Learning to look at ourselves and others through God's filter of grace keeps us in alignment with heaven's vision. Envisioning our future with tools such as vision boards and vision statements can help us focus on our hope-filled future as well as our divine destiny.

VISUALIZING THE VICTORY

God chooses many ways to communicate with us. Speaking through His Word, our circumstances, and other people are some such ways. The Holy Spirit can also reveal specific pictures, visions, and dreams to us at times. Throughout Scripture, we find many examples of God revealing His vision to others. Similarly, as we begin to envision our future, using our spiritual sight and imagination, we will be more apt to discover the plans and purposes we were designed to pursue.

There is a specific and unique vision and mission that God has in mind for us. As we continue to refine our spiritual sight, taking steps of faith along the way, our supernatural vision will come into focus.

We can trust that the Holy Spirit will continue to reveal and empower us to pursue that divine vision. Paul rejoiced that he did not live his life in vain or work without purpose. He continued to passionately pursue the purpose Jesus had for him (Philippians 3:12-14). Goals, dreams, and visions that we pursue with and for the Lord are never useless (1 Corinthians 15:58). We don't have to fulfill these visions alone either. Scripture assures us that God is working in us to fulfill His good purpose (Philippians 2:13). Now *that's* something we can believe without seeing!

I find the story of Esther inspiring. She was an unlikely candidate to become the Queen of Persia. She wasn't even Persian but was an orphan. Nevertheless, God brought her out of obscurity and gave her favor with those she met. God put her in a position of influence so that *His vision* for her people, the Jews, would come to pass. God appointed and used her to help save the lives of her entire nation! Mordecai, who raised Esther, reminded her that perhaps she had been called to the kingdom to complete the very task that lay before her (Esther 4:14). If Esther hadn't stepped into her divine purpose at that moment, God might have called another to fulfill His vision of rescuing the Jewish people.

The truth is, God has allotted the times of our existence as well as the places where we live (Acts 17:26). You (and I) have been divinely placed in God's Kingdom for such a time as this. As you ignite your "super" sight to clearly focus on the vision God has for you, you will begin to understand your purpose as Esther did.

You may not be called to deliver a nation, but you can do something special for God. Just as God used Joseph in the desert and Daniel in Babylon, God can work with you and me.

One day, after Jesus had taught a large crowd, the disciples informed Him that it was getting late, and the crowd was getting hungry. They suggested Jesus send them away so they could get dinner. Jesus responded to His disciples by saying,

"You give them something to eat!" (Matthew 14:16 AMP).

The disciples protested because they only had some leftovers to offer. Nevertheless, they brought the leftovers to Jesus at His request. Jesus then gave thanks and passed out the food. As He passed the portions to the disciples, the food miraculously multiplied in their hands. The entire crowd was well fed, and extra was leftover (Matthew 14:13-21). Similarly, God will empower us to meet needs, make a difference, or solve a problem. We may think the little that we have, as did the disciples, is not enough. However, if we offer God what we do have, and give Him something to work with, He will bless it and multiply it. The key is to identify what we *do* have and not focus on what we *don't* have. We have skills, talents, gifts, passions, and resources that we can dedicate to the Lord for Him to do something amazing with.

Elisha the prophet was once approached by a widow unable to pay a looming debt. Elisha asked,

> *"How can I help you? Tell me, what do you have in your house?"* (2 Kings 4:2 NIV).

The widow told him she had nothing *"except a small jar of olive oil"* (v. 2). As she offered the oil to Elisha, an abundance of oil was supplied to her. She had enough oil to sell, pay off her debt, and live on the rest (2 Kings 4:1-7).

As we shift our attention from what we *don't* have in the physical to what we *do* have in the spiritual we will soon visualize our victories, and our mountains being removed.

I don't know about you, but when I finally see the Lord face-to-face with my heavenly eyes, I want to hear Him say, "Well done! You were faithful and trustworthy. Come join the party" (Matthew 25:21).

MOUNTAIN-MOVING SIGHT

I don't know which mountains you're facing in life right now. Perhaps it's the mountain of sickness, fear, or lack. Maybe your mountain is perfectionism, guilt, shame, or pride. It's possible your mountain involves a relationship, a role, or a job. Your mountain might be doubt, insecurity, or disappointment. Perhaps it's busyness, tiredness, or procrastination.

What are you believing for that you still haven't seen with your physical eyes? Which mountains need to go? Don't tell God how big the mountain is; tell the mountain how big your God is! **Behold the blessing that's just on the other side of that mountain!**

We all have some version of a mountain that needs to be removed from our lives. Nonetheless, we can use those mountains to exercise our faith muscles, strengthen our vocal cords, and sharpen our spiritual eyesight. These experiences prepare us to be able to overcome our giants (like David) and endure our wilderness episodes (as the Israelites).

God's vision for us is freedom and victory; a life that is no longer bound by what we see, feel, or experience; a higher lifestyle whereby we live by what we believe, not by what we see with our physical eyes; a lifestyle of operating by what we see spiritually according to the promises of God.

The path to success is rarely easy. Those who succeed in life the most are those who also failed the most. So, what about those mountains that just haven't moved yet? It can seem as if we go around the same mountain season after season. Unfortunately, we may have to live with mountains that won't move for a while. However, even if it appears as if we are walking in circles, we are actually forming a path that is leading us higher. Every circle around the mountain leads us to a higher level until we reach the summit. The peak is the place we find our most powerful perspective. It's the high place where we can soar high above any storm life throws at us! A place where God is guiding, delivering, and transforming us. That's something we can see even with our eyes shut.

I pray this book becomes a seed that has been planted in your spirit. I hope you will allow its contents to grow deep roots as you water it with the Word, worship, and prayer. I pray that you continue to walk by faith and not by physical sight alone. As you fix your spiritual gaze on the things unseen, I hope God's vision and purpose for you become clearer. May you envision your future with God, and may the Holy Spirit continue to guide and teach you as only He can.

---

1. Tozer, The Purpose of Man: Designed to Worship.

Acknowledgements

Utmost thanks and praise to my Lord and Savior Jesus Christ for His amazing love, mercy, and grace. It has been an honor and an adventure writing with Him. It's my heartfelt desire that this book brings glory to Him.

Thank you, my loving husband Scott, for always encouraging and believing in me. I thank God for bringing you into my life.

Many thanks to my family, friends, and the Vineyard Church community for their prayers and support. May this book bless you as much as you have blessed me.

Much credit and thanks to my editor, Abbey McLaughlin, for being a timely godsend. Thanks to Miblart for collaborating on a beautiful cover design.

I can never thank the following Christian teachers and ministries enough for having such a tremendous influence on my life: Joyce Meyer, Kenneth E. Hagin, Keith Moore, Robert Morris, Sid Roth, Steve Backlund, Bill Johnson, Bethel Music, and Upper Room Dallas.

Appendix - Resources

DECLARATIONS

Use the following declaration statements to help further your spiritual vision. They will also equip you with scriptural truths regarding these eight elements of Kingdom vision:

- Purpose

- Position

- Presence

- Passion

- Perspective

- Power

- Provision

- Peace

Note: These are paraphrased statements based on the Bible and are not direct biblical quotes.

IGNITING YOUR SUPER SIGHT

The Lord can reveal Himself to me in visions and speak to me in dreams. (Num 12:6, Acts 2:17)

I see and recognize the new things God is doing in my life. (Isa 43:19)

I believe I will see God's goodness here in this place. (Ps 27:13)

I open my eyes to see the wonderful things in God's word. (Ps 119:18)

I will raise my eyes to the hills and mountains. (Ps 121:1)

My eyes have been opened to see and recognize Jesus. (Luke 24:31)

The way I look at things is being transformed by God's word. (Rom 12:2)

With an unveiled face, I am beholding and reflecting the glory of the Lord and becoming more like Him by the Holy Spirit. (2 Cor 3:18)

I focus on the eternal unseen realm. (2 Cor 4:18)

The eyes of my heart have been enlightened to see the inheritance and power I have been called into. (Eph 1:18)

AUTHENTICATING YOUR PURPOSE

The plans of the Lord will stand firm forever, the purposes of His heart to all generations. (Ps 33:11)

The Lord's purpose and plans will prevail and succeed in my life. (Prov 19:21)

I am assured by knowing that all things are fitting into a plan for my good according to God's purpose. (Rom 8:28)

God has created me in Christ Jesus for good works that were prepared for me beforehand. (Eph 2:10)

I'm convinced that God, who began the good work within me, will continue His work until it is finished and completed on the day that Christ returns. (Phil 1:6)

God is energizing and enabling me to desire and to fulfill His chosen purpose. (Phil 2:13)

I will stand, full and complete, in the whole will of God. (Col 4:12)

God has saved me and called me with a holy calling, not according to my works, but according to His own purpose and grace, which was given to me in Christ Jesus before time began. (2 Tim 1:9)

God will equip me with every good thing to do His will and work in me through Jesus Christ to accomplish what is pleasing to Him. (Heb 13:21)

DIRECTING YOUR POSITION

I am the head, not the tail. I am above, not beneath. I am blessed wherever I am. (Deut 28:13)

The Lord shall guide me continually. (Isa 58:11)

My steps are directed and established by the Lord. He delights in my way. (Ps 37:23)

In all my ways I recognize and acknowledge God, and He directs my steps. (Prov 3:6)

God has raised me up and seated me in the heavenly realm with Christ Jesus. (Eph 2:6)

God has delivered me from the power of darkness and brought me into the kingdom of His Son. (Col 1:13)

I've been buried with Christ in baptism and have been raised together with Him in faith. (Col 2:12)

I am led by the Spirit of God, so I am a child of God. (Rom 8:14)

I am a chosen person for God to possess. God has brought me out of darkness into the light. (I Pet 2:9)

I humble myself under God's mighty hand, so at the proper time He will exalt me. (I Pet 5:6)

HOSTING GOD'S PRESENCE

I am strong and courageous, not afraid or dismayed, because the Lord my God is with me wherever I go. (Josh 1:9)

The Lord is in my midst, a warrior bringing victory. He creates calm with His love and rejoices over me with singing. (Zeph 3:17)

Jesus is with me always, even to the end of this time. (Matt 28:20)

My body is a temple of the Holy Spirit who is within me. I am not my own. (1 Cor 6:19)

I am not the one living now—it is Christ living in me. I still live in my body, but I live by faith in the Son of God. (Gal 2:20)

Christ lives in my heart through faith. (Eph 3:17)

Christ in me is my hope of glory. (Col 1:27)

I am a partaker of the divine nature. (2 Pet 1:4)

I am victorious because the One who is in me is greater than the one who is in the world. (1 John 4:4)

I open the door of my heart to Jesus. He comes in and we eat together. (Rev 3:20)

FINDING PASSION

The Lord loves me with everlasting love and continues to show me His kindness. (Jer 31:3)

I love others as Jesus loves me. People know I'm a believer through my love. (John 13:34-35)

God's love has been abundantly poured out within my heart through the Holy Spirit. (Rom 5:5)

And I am convinced that nothing can ever separate me from God's love. (Rom 8:38)

I will let love be my only debt. If I love others, I have done all that the law demands. (Rom 13:8)

I do everything in love, motivated and inspired by God's love for me. (1 Cor 16:14)

Because of God's great love and mercy, He gave me life together with Christ. (Eph 2:4-5)

Christ dwells in my heart through faith. I am deeply rooted and grounded in love. (Eph 3:17)

I live a life of love, following Jesus' example. (Eph 5:2)

God's love has reached its goal in me. While I am in this world, I am like Jesus. (1 Jn 4:17)

APPLYING ETERNAL PERSPECTIVE

I desire first and foremost God's kingdom and righteousness and all the things I need will be provided for me. (Matt 6:33)

Rather than conforming to the world, I am being transformed by renewing my mind according to God's word and will. (Rom 12:2)

God is faithful and not will allow me to be tested more than I can endure. He will also make a way for me to escape! (I Cor 10:13)

I walk and live by faith, not by sight or appearance. (2 Cor 5:7)

I recognize what is important, excellent, and valuable, that I may be pure and without offense in the day of Christ. (Phil 1:10)

I will keep focusing on the goal, where the prize waiting for me is the upward call of God in King Jesus. (Phil 3:14)

I am learning how to be content and undisturbed in whatever circumstance I find myself. (Phil 4:11)

Christ gives me the strength I need to do whatever I must do. (Phil 4:13)

I fix my attention and set my mind on higher things, not on things that are only on earth. (Col 3:2)

I am getting rid of everything that distracts or impedes me as I run my race, looking at Jesus, the Author and Finisher of my faith. (Heb 12:1-2)

WALKING IN POWER

The Lord gives me strength when I am tired and more power when I feel weak. (Isa 40:29)

The Holy Spirit is in me, so I have received power and ability to be a witness for Jesus. (Acts 1:8)

God's grace is enough for me. His power and strength are effective and perfected in my weakness. (2 Cor 12:9)

I pray that I understand the incredible greatness of God's power in and for me as I believe. (Eph 1:19)

Out of His unlimited resources, God is empowering me with inner strength through His Spirit. (Eph 3:16)

God is able to do far beyond what I can ask or imagine by His power working in me. (Eph 3:20)

I have the strength to do all things in Christ who empowers me. (Phil 4:13)

I am strengthened with all power so that I can endure everything and have patience. (Col 1:11)

God has not given me a spirit of fear, but of power, love, and a sound mind. (2 Tim 1:7)

God's divine power has given me everything I need to live and serve Him. (2 Pet 1:3)

ENVISIONING THE PROVISION

The Lord is my shepherd. There is nothing that I lack. (Ps 23:1)

I seek the Lord, so I don't lack any good thing. (Ps 34:10)

I am happy and blessed as I trust the Lord. (Ps 84:12)

God will abundantly bless me with provision and satisfy me with food. (Ps 132:15)

As I seek and desire God's Kingdom first, all I need is provided. (Matt 6:33)

I give to others, and with the measure I give I will receive. (Luke 6:38)

God brings grace, favor, and blessings to me, so I have everything I need and can do more good things. (2 Cor 9:8)

I don't get tired of doing what is good, because at the right time I will reap a great harvest. (Gal 6:9)

God has blessed me with every spiritual blessing from heaven in Christ. (Eph 1:3)

God will abundantly supply all I ever need. (Phil 4:19)

ACCESSING PEACE

I am settled with God. I am at peace with Him and good comes to me. (Job 22:21)

You, Lord, will keep me in perfect peace as my mind is focused on You. (Isa 26:3)

The Lord gives strength to me and blesses me with peace. (Ps 29:11)

When I please the Lord, He will convert my enemies to peace. (Prov 16:7)

Jesus has given me His peace. I am not troubled, afraid, agitated, or disturbed. (John 14:27)

I have perfect peace in Jesus. Although I may have stress and frustration in the world, I am brave and confident because Jesus has overcome the world. (John 16:33)

I am filled with joy and peace as I believe, and the Holy Spirit empowers me with hope. (Rom 15:13)

I'm not anxious or worried about anything. I ask God for what I need and experience God's supernatural peace. (Phil 4:6-7)

I will let the peace of Christ control my heart and will be thankful. (Col 3:15)

May the Lord of Peace always give me peace in every way. (2 Thess 3:16)

SPIRITUAL VISION CHECKLIST

Use this checklist to help determine if any of the eight elements of divine spiritual vision(s) are present.

KINGDOM VISION SHOULD:

✤

- ◯ Authenticate your PURPOSE.
- ◯ Direct your POSITION.
- ◯ Encourage God's PRESENCE.
- ◯ Ignite your PASSION.
- ◯ Apply eternal PERSPECTIVE.
- ◯ Include Holy Spirit POWER.
- ◯ Require divine PROVISION.
- ◯ Bring supernatural PEACE.

OUR VISION BOARD

Here is the vision board that Scott and I created. May it inspire you as you make yours!

AN IMPORTANT QUESTION

Are you, by chance, reading this book but have never accepted Jesus Christ as your Lord and Savior? Did you know that you can begin today? The Bible tells us that if we declare aloud that Jesus is Lord and believe in our hearts that God raised Him from the dead, then we will be saved.

To be "saved" means to be rescued from spiritual death and its consequences. In the Greek language, to be saved is the word *"sozo"* and it means to be saved, healed, delivered, and made whole.

Take some time now, or in the next few days, to tell your loving Father in heaven:

> *"I believe that Jesus is the Christ, the Son of the Living God, and my personal Savior. Take my life, Lord, and do something with it! In Jesus' name, I pray. Amen."*

Be sure to share this good news with someone! Get connected with a local church. Start studying God's Word for yourself. Jesus will do things in your life that you never even imagined!

A PERSONAL FAVOR

Now that you've finished reading this book, it would be a huge favor to me, and future readers, if you left some feedback on Amazon. It would be a blessing knowing you read the whole book and shared your honest experience with the world. You can post a review on Amazon by visiting: vision2victory.org/ReviewSightBook or by simply scanning the QR code.

LOOKING FOR MORE?

Then subscribe at vision2victory.org/join to get free downloads, ministry updates, insider tips, and exclusive offers.

www.ingramcontent.com/pod-product-compliance
Lightning Source LLC
Chambersburg PA
CBHW070713130626
46553CB00005B/1963